Environmental Personhood

This book examines the increasingly widespread movement to recognise the environment as a legal person.

Several countries have now recognised that nature, or parts of nature, have juristic personhood. In this book, the concept of legal personhood and its incidents are interrogated to determine whether this is, or could be, a positive contribution to modern environmental problems. Surveying historical and current positions on the juristic concept of legal personhood, the book engages recent legislation and case law to consider the attempt in several countries to vest personhood in rivers, river basins and ecosystems. Comparing approaches in a range of countries – including New Zealand, India, Ecuador, the United States and Australia – the book addresses the methods employed, the purported aims, the mechanisms for enforcement and the entrenchment of legal protections. Throughout, the book elicits the difficult relationship between a historically anthropocentric idea of personhood and its extension beyond the human; concluding that the attribution of personhood to the environment is an important, but limited, contribution to environmental sustainability.

Accessibly written, this book will appeal to scholars, students and others with interests in environmental law, environmental science and public policy, and ecology more generally.

Francine Rochford is Associate Professor at La Trobe University, Melbourne, Australia.

Part of the
NEW TRAJECTORIES IN LAW
series

Series editors
Adam Gearey, Birkbeck College, University of London
Prabha Kotiswaran, Kings College London
Colin Perrin, Commissioning Editor, Routledge
Mariana Valverde, University of Toronto

For information about the series and details of previous and forthcoming titles, see
https://www.routledge.com/New-Trajectories-in-Law/book-series/NTL

A GlassHouse Book

Environmental Personhood

New Trajectories in Law

Francine Rochford

Routledge
Taylor & Francis Group
a GlassHouse Book

First published 2024
by Routledge
4 Park Square, Milton Park, Abingdon, Oxon OX14 4RN

and by Routledge
605 Third Avenue, New York, NY 10158

Routledge is an imprint of the Taylor & Francis Group, an informa business

A GlassHouse book

British Library Cataloguing-in-Publication Data
A catalogue record for this book is available from the British Library

Library of Congress Cataloging-in-Publication Data
Names: Rochford, Francine, author.
Title: Environmental personhood: new trajectories in law / Francine
Rochford.
Description: Abingdon, Oxon [UK]; New York, NY: Routledge, 2024. |
Series: New trajectories in law | Includes bibliographical references
and index.
Identifiers: LCCN 2023047827 (print) | LCCN 2023047828 (ebook) | ISBN
9781032482811 (hardback) | ISBN 9781032482828 (paperback) | ISBN
9781003388272 (ebook)
Subjects: LCSH: Environmental law, International. | Persons (International
law) | Juristic persons.
Classification: LCC K3585 .R625 2024 (print) | LCC K3585 (ebook) | DDC
344.04/6--dc23/eng/20231012
LC record available at https://lccn.loc.gov/2023047827
LC ebook record available at https://lccn.loc.gov/2023047828

ISBN: 9781032482811 (hbk)
ISBN: 9781032482828 (pbk)
ISBN: 9781003388272 (ebk)

DOI: 10.4324/9781003388272

Typeset in Sabon
by Deanta Global Publishing Services, Chennai, India

Contents

Contents

Chapter 1

Introduction

Ubi jus ibi remedium [where there is a right there is a remedy]

The turn of the century has seen a concerted programme of advocacy, legislative change and litigation to repose 'legal personhood' in the environment, or aspects thereof. This is intended to create new legal avenues of protection for the environment, but also to reposition the environment in the landscape of rights and obligations created by law. *Environmental Personhood: New Trajectories in Law* addresses this movement. It analyses the idea of legal (or juristic) personhood, tracing its origin, the complex meanings attached to the term, and the particular social and legal contexts in which personhood creates strategic advantages in campaigns for environmental protection. This movement, like the litigation strategy addressing climate change, reaches into the heart of legal philosophy as well as turning on alternative views of the status of international law.

This book unravels some of the skeins of contestation, including the problematisation of power in legal frameworks, the historical and conceptual idea of the person in law, the enlightenment separation of science and superstition, reason and affect, the separation of religion and the state, the basis of legal authority in unitary and pluralist legal systems, the role of law and the limitations inherent in developed legal systems through the separation of legislative and judicial powers. However, its focus will be on the mechanisms for implementing rights in nature and the motivations for reposing personhood in the environment. Using five case studies in different jurisdictions, the book will demonstrate that full personhood is not the typical outcome of constitutional, legislative or judicial reform, but that the models of recognition are usually modified versions of protections already afforded. However, the strategic advocacy behind personhood claims carries its own consequences, including the shaping of public opinion, the creation of precedent, the integration

DOI: 10.4324/9781003388272-1

of new concepts into the law and the remapping of meanings in culture and law.

Reposing incidents of personhood in non-human, interacting forms with unclear and changing boundaries (Clark et al., 2018, p. 797) and no capacity to assert legal rights and duties on their own behalf creates both conceptual and practical difficulties for enforcement. With this in mind, the traditional concept of legal personhood and its incidents in this context will be interrogated, with a view to determining whether reposing legal personhood in natural elements is a useful solution or partial solution to modern environmental problems; or whether, indeed, 'personhood' here is being used in an entirely different sense.

It is important to note what this book is *not*. It is not an assessment of political positions. This cannot be achieved within the parameters of this series. Although the environmental critique of the existing institutional arrangements tends to align with the 'left leaning' end of the political spectrum, and much of the language and many of the ideas inherent in the personhood debate have their origins in various left positions, this account will, so far as is possible, summarise extant views which have had legal purchase. Thus, it is not a detailed account of the philosophical aspects of the debate on legal personhood. Nor is it a review of the concept of personhood in every legal system. Again, that would not be achievable. Rather, this is a pragmatic derivation of the legal authority behind environmental personhood claims, concentrating on the jurisdictions in which the modern movement has had the most purchase. What will be attempted is an insight into the conceptual framework of the debate, the drivers and strategies deployed by the movement for environmental personhood and the way in which these strategies have played out in some representative jurisdictions. It will become clear that there are common features to attempts to deploy personhood claims, including the critical stance adopted in relation to 'power' in law and, accordingly, the legitimacy of law, and the incorporation of indigenous views to approach pluralism in legal systems that speak to longstanding and unresolved debates in law. There are also deep disparities between the different manifestations of personhood, which reach into the normative basis of the asserted rights.

Many of the organising themes of *legal* arguments for reposing personhood in nature can be traced to the critical legal studies (CLS) movement, which arose in the United States in the 1970s. This movement had a marked effect on legal education and scholarship, particularly after the 1980s. Whilst perhaps 'its founders never meant it to become an ongoing school of thought or genre of writing' (Clark, 1994, p. 56), the determination to address the implicit power biases effected and maintained through traditional legal mechanisms and techniques has proved resilient. The analytic techniques of CLS purport to identify and critique injustice in current legal institutions and methods, including in the claim to equal treatment before the law and the claim to rationality in law itself. The movement also, however, posits a utopian vision. Several themes arising from claims to personhood in nature have emerged from the CLS movement and its successors – critical race theory, critical feminist theory and now ecocritical views of law. What Chowdhury describes as the 'activist premise' (Chowdhury, 2018, p. 21) has been naturalised in legal scholarship, contributing to acceptance of the truism that 'law is politics', anathematising the role of power in the law, highlighting the indeterminism of legal rules and the blurring of the distinction between public and private law (Chowdhury, 2018, p. 20), and the 'universalization projects' of ideologues (Kennedy, 2002, p. 188).

The CLS movement did not arise in a vacuum; it was a broadly left/Marxist movement, and there remain elements of what is termed 'cultural Marxism' in the literature around environmental personhood. This is so unsurprising as to be orthodox in modern academic legal discourse. Law is a construct, an invention of people to order people. Law and legal institutions are visible manifestations of power and are experienced in different ways by different groups. Whilst formally most modern law in a particular jurisdiction applies equally to everybody (and so Iustitia may be blindfolded); in practice law will have a more onerous impact on some than on others. Indigenous peoples in colonised societies will often be adversely affected by modern law and legal systems, so a blind justice actually perpetuates injustice. For most legal systems this has resulted in the law actively 'taking sides' to address long-term situational disadvantage. Modern efforts to remedy the ongoing effects of colonialism fall into this category. That these efforts undermine features valued by a conservative legal system (elements such as property rights and freedom and certainty of contract) is considered, on balance, appropriate given the 'higher end' served – real equality and real justice. This may not, however, be a sufficiently ambitious aim; some scholars call for a more literal interpretation of Marxist tenets and a more direct attack on what is described as 'the repressive commodity fetishism of Western legalism' and compared unflatteringly with 'the perspective of Indigenous people who thrived for millennia' (Agozino, 2018) without such fetishism. Because law is, under traditional Marxist ideology, meant to 'wither away' with the state, 'Marxists do not consider the role law might play in post-capitalist society' (Sypnowich, 1987, p. 305), and it is unsurprising that the occasional logical cul-de-sac would arise through the 'capture' of and submission of nature to the logic of law.

Similarly, the CLS movement was ambivalent to the idea of 'rights' given its leftist/Marxist roots, as rights discourse tended to be individualistic rather than communitarian – 'Marx critiqued individual rights as rights of egoistic beings, arguing that beneath the veneer of "liberal rights for all", existed a highly unequal and inegalitarian society' (Wahi, 2022). However, this ambivalence has been replaced by an enthusiastic embrace of rights discourse; accelerated, no, doubt, by the useful malleability of the term itself. The term 'rights' in positivist legal discourse, as premised on distinct legal categories and enforceable by legal institutions, does not have anything like the same meaning as the term 'rights' from a utopian perspective. However, as Kennedy (2002, p. 188) argues, rights discourse can be used in argument to convert the interests of a group, by narrative means, into a universal interest and thence to a universal right. It is critical to the understanding of the discussion about ecosystem rights arising from personhood that these multiple meanings of 'rights' are acknowledged. It is also important to understand the logic of rights in each of those meanings, and the way in which rights discourse is deployed in argument. The rapidly developing case law in environmental personhood provides a point of intersection between the positivist rights framework and the deployment of rights discourse from the critical perspective. However, as we will see, extensive translative steps occur to enable critical understandings of rights to be argued in traditional legal frameworks.

Structure of the text

This chapter commences with a brief account of the environmental concerns prompting recognition of this new legal framework. These concerns range from point source and nonpoint source pollution, through problems of overallocation of environmental resources, to the systemic alteration of the composition of the atmosphere. The chapter will then summarise the motivations behind legal advocacy for legal recognition of parts of the ecosystem with legal personhood and the various legal incidents attaching to recognition as a person. It discusses recent legislation and case law in several jurisdictions including Ecuador, India, New Zealand, Australia and the United States, which assert or confer forms of legal personhood in elements of the environment. It will place these legal developments in the context of sustainable development and the various legal strategies deployed to address sustainability, and in the context of ecocentric approaches to environmental concerns. The introductory chapter will then set out the structure of the remaining chapters.

Chapter 2 will consider what is meant by 'legal person' from the legal perspective, the modern incidents attaching to legal personhood and the way in which some conceptions of environmental personhood favour the anthropocentric construction of sustainable development. Chapter 3 consists of case studies from several jurisdictions that have reposed protections approaching legal personhood, or cognate recognition, in the environment or parts thereof. Case studies from Ecuador, New

Zealand, India, the United States and Australia will be considered in their legal and historical context, the conceptualisations of personhood adopted and the extent of the protections afforded. The legal sources of personhood range from national constitutions, legislation, case law and treaties. Chapter 4 builds upon the case studies using traditional legal analytical frameworks, isolating key tensions between the strategy for posited forms of environmental personhood and understandings and values in legal systems. The concluding chapter will develop an argument for coherence in approaches to the legal protection of the environment.

What is the problem, and why is this the solution?

Earth's apocalypse and hard choices

One of the primary motivations for acknowledging forms of personhood other than human personhood is the sense of ecosystem crisis arising from anthropocentric utilisation of the environment, and the insight that ecosystem destruction affects both human and non-human interests. Research indicates a widening range of climate change impacts, justifying the disruption of traditional advocacy measures. Litigation has become part of the arsenal of protesters and has 'emerged as a plausible way to prompt enhanced action on climate change litigation' (Benoit, 2023, p. 233).

Litigation occurs in the context of state-based judicial systems applying laws with sometimes ancient restrictions on access to justice. To utilise litigation techniques instead of, or along with, agitation for legislative reform raises questions of legal personhood and standing that may be premised on fundamental understandings of the law. Using private law techniques to reach beyond state boundaries to trace environmental impacts also challenges the traditional reach of the jurisdiction of a court, which takes its authority from the state, traditionally interpreted. The ongoing project represented by the United Nations, which explicitly addresses environmental protection in various documents, accentuates this problem. United Nations declarations are largely political documents and are of little more than normative force until passed into local law or adopted by adventurous local courts (Kerwin, 1983). The growing domestic influence of institutions such as the World Trade Organisation exacerbates the concerns of some commentators who suggest that 'sovereignty is threatened by the ongoing expansion of global governance' (Raustiala, 2003, p. 842). For the purposes of this text, I will not be unravelling the many contested strains of sovereignty but considering state sovereignty from its legal perspective. State law is typically enforceable only within state borders. Extra-territorial operation requires political and administrative arrangements between states. State laws and legal systems are created, funded and maintained by individual states and, broadly speaking, maintain their legitimacy through techniques that carry cogency within that state. Thus, international instruments such as United Nations declarations have no legal force unless adopted by local jurisdictions. However, they do have political and strategic force and need to be considered as part of the language of environmental advocacy.

That the planet has and is continuing to experience environmental problems is not open to serious debate. Whilst it could be said that some of these problems are local or regional, in the sense that their effects are contained within a small area, others have the potential to cause, or have already caused, catastrophic ecosystem destruction, decline or irreversible change. Moreover, even in cases of 'contained' environmental damage, the effects may move beyond one entity or system. Environmental advocates stress the connectedness of ecosystems and seek regulation of human activities to mitigate or remove the potential for harm. From a jurisdictional perspective, this means that law, which is constrained in geographical terms, artificially constrains actions to cure environmental wrongs to part of an ecosystem. This is of particular significance where environmental elements (such as rivers) cross national borders. National laws that affect one part of the river cannot reach the part of the river over the border.

Increasing and increasingly dense populations increase the potential for ecosystem damage. As this will often result in damage to humans or human interests, laws in developed legal systems will typically regulate activities that damage people. For instance, heavy metal contamination resulting from urbanisation and industrialisation is considered one of the most hazardous pollutants (Govind & Madhuri, 2014) and may result from ingestion, respiration or skin contact. It may be spread by dust, drinking water, ingestion of meat in which bioaccumulation of toxins has occurred or by growing vegetables in contaminated soils. Methods of addressing these interactions can be seen in the common law tort of nuisance, planning laws and environmental protection laws at various levels of government. These legal instruments may be supplemented by other non-legal mechanisms, such as industry codes of conduct and best practice guidelines, and the operation of the market is also relied upon to facilitate consumer preference for environmentally sustainable production, transport and packaging. It should be recognised, therefore, that traditional law, arising both in common law and legislation, already regulates many of the actions that damage the environment.

Environmental risks are not always understood, and ecosystem connectivity is often imperfectly appreciated. This insight is also capable of being brought into existing legal mechanisms. The incorporation of the 'precautionary principle' in land use planning and environmental law is an example. This principle, typically included in legislation relating to land use decisions, developed in Europe over the 1970s and was broadly recognised following the 1992 United Nations Conference on Environment and Development. It is frequently adopted into national legislation by incorporation of the Rio Declaration on Environment and Development (United Nations, 1992), the United Nations Framework Convention on Climate Change (1992) or the Convention on Biological Diversity (1992). In Europe, it is incorporated in the 1992 Maastricht Treaty (European Union, 1992). Principle 15 requires that lack of full scientific certainty on the threat of serious or irreversible damages 'shall not be used as a reason for postponing cost-effective measures to prevent environmental degradation' (Rio Declaration, 1992). The principle, when brought into domestic legislation, guides administrative decision-making and forms part of a set of policy arguments to be acknowledged or incorporated in decision-making at all levels of government.

This and other matters, which a decision-maker is required to consider, will often be specified in legislation as interpreted by the judiciary, and typically avenues are available for review of administrative decisions through litigation (this is the province of what is conventionally termed 'administrative law'). Broadly, however, there may be considerable scope for decision-makers to apply different weighting to different factors, and there will often be a discretionary element. A conjunction of circumstances may require a choice to be made between two values or goals. In that instance, in the absence of an overriding moral argument such as may prevail in theocracies, decisions will be made on the basis of the balance of perceived social benefit. This balance is calculated in an information deficit not entirely ameliorated by the precautionary principle; in many cases, human activity is intended to produce positive outcomes but has unanticipated effects, and those effects may not be clear until many years after the date of the activity. In these circumstances, even with the most benign or even beneficent intentions, there may be environmental harm. Even if they are understood the level of impact may be considered to be less significant than the societal 'good' to be realised by the activity, so a decision will seek the lesser of two acknowledged evils. Examples of this are frequently reported: in Australia, the development of alternative energies in the form of wind turbines to replace fossil fuels is claimed to threaten a wet sclerophyll forest (Cater, 2023). In the United States, the production of biofuel is argued to be 'killing endangered species and harming the environment' (Perkins, 2023). There are many examples of unintended consequences that should act as a caution to those arguing for a view that there will be a single view emanating from diverse environmental persons, any more that there is a single view emanating from different humans. If we factor into this that the 'voice' of the environment must be translated through human interlocutors, we are faced with interpretations not significantly clearer than we have today.

Value constructs inform all decision-making, and the interests of humans have tended to take priority (and, significantly, the interests of the *greater number* of humans will also often take priority over the interests of the lesser number). Land clearing for agriculture, ranging from deliberate government policy framed as a legislative requirement of land ownership to the illegally cleared ground supporting subsistence agriculture, has resulted in global deforestation. Individual, state or national priorities to produce food (or maintain an export economy or retain the capacity to produce food to reduce the risks posed by war or other logistical or supply issues) will be balanced against the more vague or distant threats posed by deforestation. In the American West, the destruction of 'apex' predators such as grey wolves to preserve domestic animals resulted in an explosion in the number of native ruminant and nonnative species and consequent ecosystem destruction. In Australia, the 5300-kilometre dingo barrier fence protects sheep from the predations of dingoes; but, in excluding the dingo, it leaves small native animals vulnerable to other, introduced predators such as foxes and cats (Rees et al., 2019). As further study occurs more complex adaptations and interactions are observed. In the United States, 'rewilding' programmes focusing on federal lands propose changes in land use to retire grazing allotments (Ripple et al., 2022, p. 933). The benefits of rewilding are now considered to outweigh the benefits of food production and other social and economic goals, but the achievement of those benefits necessitates the payment of compensation to those relinquishing grazing permits (Ripple et al., 2022, p. 934), shifting public moneys from other public purposes. Similar rewilding projects are occurring in Norway (wolves), Scotland (sea eagles), Spain (wild boar) and Italy (wild boar) (Duckett et al., 2022), Switzerland, Germany and Poland (Eurasian lynx) (Boitani & Linnell, 2015) and Australia (dingo) (Kingsford et al., 2021). Translocation of bears has occurred in the Italian Alps, the Pyrenees and central Austria (Boitani & Linnell, 2015, p. 70). The degree of risk to grazing stock in areas beyond the range of the reintroduction of predators similarly requires an assignment of risks and priorities. The risk assignment will occur differently between those whose lives or stock are at risk (Duckett et al., 2022) and those who take a system-wide approach to ecosystem risk and may not only be a function of economic loss (Zahl-Thanem et al., 2020). In Italy, there have been several instances of bear attacks, including fatal attacks (Ghiglione, 2023, Kirby, 2023; Hardach, 2023). In Australia, the conservation of purebred dingo populations has come into conflict with risks to humans and a financial benefit of tourism at K'gari (formerly Fraser Island) (Allen et al., 2015; Couper, 2023).

We can see that decision-making on matters requiring a balance between human *needs* (as well as wants) and ecosystem needs will almost inevitably prioritise human needs, and to an extent is almost inevitably utilitarian in the sense that it will prioritise the highest number of affected people, and more relevantly in situations of crisis will prioritise present over future needs. In the most obvious instance, a single event requires a triage response, allocating comparative value to two incompatible goals – most clearly exemplified by the destruction of an individual animal of a threatened species because that animal has killed or is dangerous to human life. These decisions are also required at a system level. Land clearing to manage fire risk is now permitted in many parts of Australia, reversing or mitigating previous policies preventing the destruction of native vegetation. A link between the 'cool burning' practices of Indigenous peoples and the requirements of the evolved Australian landscape has prompted the utilisation of fire in land management practices. In the Australian government's response to the overextraction of water in the Murray Darling Basin, competing priorities are conceptualised as a balance between environmental, social and economic uses of water. The correction of overallocation uses a largely market-based tool, but when water availability becomes critically low (as it can in the Australian environment), s 86A(1) of the *Water Act 2007* (Cth) prioritises critical human needs, including the utilisation of large engineering projects to take store water from reservoirs and transport it from water-scarce areas to metropolitan Melbourne. Other systemic approaches to balance human and other ecosystem needs use market tools or concepts: the engagement of 'ecosystem services' categories and valuations enables policymakers to place values on unmodified or slightly modified wilderness and compare these with extractive or productive uses. Acknowledgement of value in carbon storage, air quality and freshwater provision, biodiversity and wildlife support, and recreation and other social benefits (see, for instance, Cerqueira et al., 2015) creates an anthropocentric valuation rather than one based on inherent worth (if we accept that 'worth' is at all compatible with an ecocentric view).

Whether those decisions are made by an individual (to clear land to grow food, to extract water, to burn fuel to keep warm) or by a nation-state (to enact policies to increase agricultural production, to create domestic water or irrigation schemes, to approve mining for fossil fuels), the question in the end is always one of the priorities. In Western nation-states, the human aspect of the decision is often concealed by the scale of the project, but each decision has impacts at an individual level and occasionally the impact will threaten life, or at least livelihood. Thus, in a political and legal system in which human life tends to take priority in instances of short- to medium-term resource competition, the priorities of non-human nature, or elements of nature, seem inevitably to be relegated to a lesser position. This is the context in which the debate surrounding the legal personhood of nature is placed.

Priorities are a well-established concept in legal systems. Common law adjudicates between holders of incompatible rights all the time. The most clearly enunciated examples of this arise in property law, where legitimate rights may exist simultaneously in the same parcel of land. The law gives precedence to legal rights on the basis of historically developed priority rules, often eventually codified. Where different uses of land conflict, long-held common law principles of nuisance apply. The tort of 'nuisance' is a creation of the common law and applies where the actions of one occupier of land unreasonably diminish the comfort or amenity of another's interests in land. For instance, if one landowner's use of land emits fumes, smoke or noxious chemicals which damage the property or reduce the amenity of a neighbour, an action in nuisance may be available to obtain an order to restrict the harmful actions. The tort balances legitimate uses of land against the legitimate interests of others who may be affected by that use on the basis of the so-called 'calculus of nuisance', which weighs the locality of the property, the time, duration, frequency and extent of the activity constituting the nuisance, the availability of alternatives to the defendant's activities and the motive of the defendant in carrying out the activity. All of these factors are to be considered in light of the overall rule of give and take. System-wide and fundamental changes, such as those proposed by those advocating personhood for nature, override these common law rules, typically by legislation, superimposing a novel and untested set of concepts, rights and priorities. Where this occurs, as for instance in the case of legislated planning laws, public consultation is typically required by the legislation and that consultation will frequently involve consideration of environmental interests. In developed legal systems, therefore, there are existing opportunities for consideration of environmental values, and these opportunities are contained in long-established and legitimated procedures. For advocates of environmental personhood, the persuasive narrative must therefore address the disturbances to long-held understandings of relative rights.

Standing for nature

Aside from political advocacy, priority claims can be resolved through formal dispute resolution – in legal proceedings. For environmental advocates, this has been seen as a major obstacle to significant environmental reform. In many legal systems there are complex rules of 'standing' which determine whether a person has sufficient interest in a matter to bring legal proceedings. Standing (or *locus standi*) rules are various, depending on the type of legal action and the jurisdiction, but they once again are an expression of balancing rights and outcomes. Rules of standing need to balance access to justice and the need to hold wrongdoers to account against public costs and the capacity of a judicial system and the risks to the administration of justice if it were overburdened with claims by parties with no personal interest in the outcome of the proceedings. Standing rules may prevent a person from bringing a legal action merely on environmental grounds and 'neither trees nor animals have standing' (*Robinson v. Waitakere City Council,* 2010, p. 23). The early work of Christopher Stone (1972) from which modern advocacy for environmental personhood is often traced, focused on the issue of standing. His arguments were grounded in the belief that existing laws failed to protect the environment and that conceptualising nature (or elements of nature) as holders of rights could provide greater protection. His later work (Stone, 2010) also recognised the legal particularity of rules of standing and the outcomes arising from the environment being acknowledged as having suffered damage *in its own right.*

There are a number of threads to this argument. It recognises that law and legal systems are a human construct and that traditional avenues for relief are ill-adapted to remediate environmental damage where it does not cause ancillary damage to humans. Stone's work was primarily based on the law of the USA and although the restrictions on the litigation of legal claims by the environment are reasonably generic to Western legal systems, generalisations are 'worthless' (*Association of Data Processing Service Organisations Inc v. Camp,* 1970). The problems of legal standing of identifying and calculating harm to the environment in its own right are fundamental issues in environmental litigation. Underlying these issues, however, a more complex patchwork of legal principles exists depending on the legal action through which relief is sought. Once we move beyond Western legal systems, the legal obstacles to protection of the inherent rights to the environment become even more problematic.

Limitations on standing are not universal and are no longer as restrictive as they were in 1972. For example, although India has acknowledged very extensive personhood rights in the environment, there is no standing issue in India as the Indian constitution allows individuals to seek redress where it is asserted that a fundamental right has been violated. Thus, issues of standing, which were the foundation of Stone's (1972) argument, have little relevance in the Indian context (Chaturvedi, 2019, p. 723). In some jurisdictions, groups of persons have had sufficient standing to bring an action to protect the environment – sometimes when their interests are considered aligned with the continued health of the environment. For instance, in *Oposa v. Department of the Environment and Natural Resources* (1994), the Supreme Court of the Philippines granted a group of children standing to sue to uphold the environmental rights of themselves and future generations. Similar strategies have been deployed in other countries with mixed success. In *Sharma v. Minister for the Environment* (2021), a decision of the Australian Federal Court at first instance held that the Commonwealth Minister for the Environment owed a common law duty of care to Australian children in the decision to approve an extension of a coal mine. Although this decision was overturned on appeal in *Minister for the Environment v. Sharma* (2022), the litigation has prompted political pressure to amend the *Climate Change Act* (Cth) to require the federal government to consider the health and wellbeing of children when making decisions under a range of Acts (Cox, 2023). In Montana, USA, a district court found held for young environmental activists, finding that environmental provisions in the Montana Constitution required that the state take measures to prevent fossil fuel emissions contributing to climate change (*Held v. State of Montana*, 2023), although the state has indicated that it will appeal. There is no doubt that there are many opportunities in the incremental processes of common law or the focused processes of legislative reform to address issues of standing.

So why personhood?

Where rights conflict, the long history of disputation catalogued in common law or pre-empted in legislation demonstrates the capacity to resolve the dispute. Where rights claims arise from personhood, however, there is a far greater potential for breach of what would now be regarded as fundamental rights. This speaks to the central issue and the fundamental value proposition to be tested in the conceptualisation of non-human personhood. Modern law (like politics) will typically value human life over other life forms and non-living elements of the environment. This value proposition is illustrated in the legal infrastructure of many systems. For instance, whereas self-defence is a legitimate excuse for killing another, the range of permitted actions in self-defence is constrained. Where a person has lost their life as a result of a person's actions in self-defence the matter may still proceed in a criminal trial, demonstrating the value placed on human life even in comparison with other human life. There are circumstances in which the value of a human life may be overridden by other values. These tend to be human versus human value ascriptions – most nation-states permit the exposure of humans (soldiers) to the possibility of death in declared war situations. In some states or nation-states, the execution of criminals is permitted. This may be legal only in cases of person-on-person violence, or murder, so that there is a direct correspondence of values. In some nation-states, the execution of persons may occur in the event of a breach of some other value, such as a matrimonial vow or religious tenet. A major ethical divide exists between those who believe that the foetus is a human and those who do not. In some belief systems where a decision must be made between the interests of the mother and that of the foetus the latter, as the most vulnerable, should prevail. In many Western legal systems, however, this view is not represented in the law, which preferences the rights of the mother. Where a dispute requires that a choice be made between the safety of a person and other values, the safety of the human person tends to be prioritised. Oppositional values may, in various legal fact situations, be manifest in the values attached to, for instance, property, liberty, the life of an animal or obligations arising from civic or contractual duty.

It is clear, from the preceding examples, that recognition of personhood in law provides a set of rights that tend to reflect contemporary ethics. Human personhood provides the highest level of legal protection because that is the societal and/or cultural value most protected. Where legal personhood has been provided to non-humans it is typically limited to a certain set of legal capacities. It is my thesis, therefore, that extending the class of legal personhood to other categories of non-humans creates issues of priority, and that it is problematic to discuss aspects of legal personhood for elements of the environment unless we are willing to answer the question – whose rights prevail? Or rather, what parameters will be applied or decision systems utilised to determine whose rights will prevail? Since the environment can't speak for itself, who is to be trusted to represent its interests, and how are these people to be selected? Some states have created, pursuant to statute, groups to enable consultation and/or decision-making in relation to these environmental elements, since they can't speak for themselves. Why are these bodies considered more appropriate than delegated authorities with more traditional ambits and subject to more traditional democratic oversight?

But we have other fundamental questions, which will become apparent in the case studies. Whereas some jurisdictions have asserted that personhood applies to Mother Earth, or nature itself (as a whole), others have elevated only parts of the environment. Some have stressed the interactivity of the different elements of the environment (not excluding humans) but have given no strategies for determining the weight to be applied to ecosystem elements where their interests might clash or be incompatible. Other than showing a clear preference for species and ecosystem functions indigenous to an area (but not indicating a temporal scope for indigeneity), the capacity for enforcement of rights is as yet undeveloped.

Strategic advocacy

The modern impetus for environmental personhood follows a deliberate and strategic path. Demos notes that it represents 'a cultural-social-political revolution in jurisprudence, and more broadly in philosophical worldview' (Demos, 2015). There is a developed programme of advocacy that aims for legislative and judicial articulation of a set of value positions in relation to environmental personhood, often (but not exclusively) in the context of amelioration of climate change. Strategic approaches can have a range of aims, overt and incidental; for instance, the aim to collapse the cultural construction of personhood as limited to human categories and uses, and a desire to undermine the forms of legal positivism that maintain the authority of the state, and to place pressure on our ontological assumptions.

This strategy is well-advanced in relation to some environmental issues: The Global Climate Litigation Report (United Nations, 2023) identified 2180 cases filed in 65 jurisdictions using various legal actions to address climate change (see, for instance, Long, 2004; Peel, 2007; Macdonald, 2011; Fournier, 2017; Peel & Osofsky, 2018; De Vito & Andreassen, 2020). Similar trends in litigation-advocacy are evident in the animal rights movement – a trend considered more closely in Chapter 2. Macdonald (2011) notes characteristics of the law that render it an attractive institution to effect desired reform – it can work as a facilitator of adaptation, since it

> confers rights and imposes obligations; provides the architecture for regulating behavior and activities, including the performance of government functions; establishes the framework for public participation in government decision making; and arbitrates and resolves disputes between the state and private individual and between individuals.
>
> (Macdonald, 2011, p. 284)

Law also acts as a barrier to the types of innovations sought in relation to environmental personhood. In the context of legal personhood, much of the infrastructure of law is premised on anthropocentrism, the centrality of human persons and interests, and much legal philosophy justifying the imposition of law relates to its role in regulating human relationships. There is a fundamental disconnect between ecocentric/biocentric models, which place humans on the same level as the rest of nature, and the utilisation of human legal frameworks. Calls for reform of basic legal principles, such as constitutional provisions, can come up against the law's legitimating infrastructure. For instance, Macdonald identifies legal requirements, such as constitutional or other obligations to compensate for acquisition of property, as 'perverse' since they have the effect of 'discouraging positive strategies or behaviours' (Macdonald, 2011, p. 287). This appears to subvert the idea of law's legitimacy, since whether or not strategies and behaviours are 'positive' is a matter to be washed through the same democratic mechanisms as the legal impediments to change. That this is a more important consideration to some (for instance, conservative lawyers), than to others will not be surprising; but given the success of the critical legal studies movement in legal academia, it bears less weight than one may think. Some advocates of radical change argue that crisis circumstances render structural legal change justifiable. This argument should be treated with caution: we should be wary of allowing authority to narrate itself into power by assertions of crisis since those assertions can be justified by a variety of situations.

Kauffman and Martin describe four pathways used by activists: '(1) norm-driven civil society pressure, (2) instrumental government action, (3) bureaucratic institutionalization, and (4) professional interpretation by judges' (Kauffman & Martin, 2017, p. 131). We can see that these strategies are interlinked and that judicial interpretation, for instance, might be sought by strategists in order to drive civil norms or prompt government action. Indeed, strategic legal advocacy has several goals; the most pertinent of these from the perspective of the environmental personhood movement are:

a. increasing the profile of the movement, potentially attracting funding, further supporters and raising the awareness of the greater population to environmental problems.
b. influencing public opinion to accept the idea of environmental personhood, which in turn places pressure on governments to change the law through legislation, funded programmes or other environmental works.
c. bringing legal action with the goal of succeeding in an individual case, creating a precedent that can be utilised in further litigation.

The use of litigation as a strategic tool has attracted the most criticism (compared with the application of pressure for legislative change). The primary point of contention is the deployment of the application of *stare decisis*, or the 'doctrine of precedent'. Stare decisis is the process by which judicial decision-making identifies the principles applied in analogous cases in higher courts in the jurisdiction and applies them to the case at issue. This is a law-making function, as courts are creating principles where none previously existed. If taken too far, *stare decisis* bypasses the more appropriate forum for law-making, and there have been many examples of courts who refuse to draw analogies too far, because decisions with wide-ranging effects are the proper role of the legislature. Modern legislative reform draws legitimacy from democratic mandate. The separation of powers doctrine, which applies to varying degrees across modern systems, supplements the veracity of the claim to legitimacy by preventing the unelected judiciary or administrative arms of government from exercising legislative tasks (and vice versa). An 'activist' judiciary risks moving beyond traditional claims to legitimacy if it exercises a legislative role. More practically, the judiciary is ill-equipped by design or resourcing to undertake the enquiries necessary to determine the impact of significant change. In adversarial systems, which are based on parties framing their own issues and presenting their own arguments, the forum is particularly ill-suited to widespread reform as the court does not have the capacity to draw upon community views or expert knowledge to assess the impact of large-scale policy change. We will return to this question in due course.

References

Agozino, B. (2018). The withering away of the law: An indigenous perspective on the decolonisation of the criminal justice system and criminology. *Journal of Global Indigeneity*, 3(1). https://ro.uow.edu.au/jgi/vol3/iss1/2

Allen, B. L., Higginbottom, K., Bracks, J. H., Davies, N., & Baxter, G. S. (2015). Balancing dingo conservation with human safety on Fraser Island: The numerical and demographic effects of humane destruction of dingoes. *Australasian Journal of Environmental Management*, 22(2), 197–215. https://doi.org/10.1080/14486563.2014.999134.

Association of Data Processing Service Organisations Inc v. Camp, (1970), 397 U.S. 150.

Benoit, M. (2023). Prompting climate change mitigation through litigation. *International and Comparative Law Quarterly*, 72(1), 233–250.

Cater, N. (2023, July 24). Is Chalumbin set to be the new Franklin Dam? *The Australian*. https://www.theaustralian.com.au/commentary/is-chalumbin -set-to-be-the-new-franklin-dam/news-story/713bbd58a15f3fc42f96a6e d4f1ce1a4

Cerqueira, Y., Navarro, L. M., Maes, J., Marta-Pedroso, C., Honrado, J. P., & Pereira, H. M. (2015). Ecosystem services: The opportunities of rewilding in Europe. In H. M. Pereira & L. M. Navarro (Eds.), *Rewilding European landscapes* (pp. 47–64). Springer Open. https://doi.org/10.1007/978-3-319 -12039-3

Chaturvedi, I. (2019). Why the Ganga should not claim a right of the river. *Water International*, 44(6–7), 719–735. https://doi.org/10.1080/02508060.2019 .1679947

Chowdhury, M., & Ali, J. (2018). Law as politics: Reflections on the critical legal studies movement. *SCLS Law Review*, 1(2), 17–21.

Clark, C., Emmanouil, N., Page, J., & Pelizzon, A. (2018). Can you hear the rivers sing: Legal personhood, ontology, and the nitty-gritty of governance. *Ecology Law Quarterly*, 45, 787.

Clark, G. J. (1994). A conversation with Duncan Kennedy. *The Advocate: The Suffolk University Law School Journal*, 24(2), 56.

Climate Change Act (Cth).

Couper, E. (2023, July 17). Woman mauled by pack of dingoes of K'gari. *The Australian.* https://www.theaustralian.com.au/nation/woman-mauled -by-pack-of-dingoes-on-kgari/news-story/0b72e6a4e1ab178402790d8 64de989dc

Cox, L. (2023, July 31). Pocock seeks to impose duty of care on Australian government over climate harm. *The Guardian.* https://www.theguardian .com/australia-news/2023/jul/31/pocock-seeks-to-impose-duty-of-care-on -australian-government-over-climate-harm

Demos, T. J. (2015). Rights of nature: The art and politics of earth jurisprudence. In T. J. Demos, A. Farquharson, & I. Aristizábal (Eds.), *Rights of nature: Art and ecology in the Americas* (pp. 1–15). Nottingham Contemporary.

De Vito, L., & Andreassen, I. S. (2020). Climate litigation in Norway. A preliminary assessment. *DPCE Online, 43*(2). https://www.dpceonline.it/ index.php/dpceonline/article/view/967

Duckett, D., Bjørkhaug, H., Mur, L. A., & Palmioli, L. (2022). New 'old' risks on the small farm: Iconic species rewilding in Europe. *Land Use Policy, 118,* 106115. https://doi.org/10.1016/j.landusepol.2022.106115

European Union (1992, February 7). Treaty on European Union, Treaty of Maastricht. *Official Journal of the European Communities C, 191,* 1–112.

Fournier, L. (2017). *The cost of inaction: The role of courts in climate change litigation.* Thesis submitted for the degree of LLM. Global Environment and Climate Change Law University of Edinburgh.

Ghiglione, D. (2023, April 12). Bear hunt after jogger killed in Italian Alps. *BBC News.* https://www.bbc.com/news/world-europe-65249457

Hardach, S. (2023, June 30). A debate over troublesome bears in the Alps shows the complex challenge of rewilding large carnivores. *BBC Future.* https://www .bbc.com/future/article/20230627-the-alpine-row-over-problem-bears

Held v. State of Montana. (2023). Cause No. CDV-2020-307 https:// climatecasechart.com/wp-content/uploads/case-documents/2023/20230814 _docket-CDV-2020-307_order.pdf

Kauffman, C. M., & Martin, P. L. (2017). Can rights of nature make development more sustainable? Why some Ecuadorian lawsuits succeed and others fail. *World Development, 92,* 130–142.

Kennedy, D. (2002). The critique of rights in critical legal studies. In W. Brown & J. Halley (Eds.), *Left legalism/left critique.* Duke University Press.

Kerwin, G. J. (1983). The role of United Nations General Assembly resolutions in determining principles of international law in United States Courts. *Duke Law Journal, 1983*(4), 876–899. https://doi.org/10.2307/1372469

Kingsford, R. T., West, R. S., Pedler, R. D., Keith, D. A., Moseby, K. E., Read, J. L., Letnic, M., Leggett, K. E. A., & Ryall, S. R. (2021). Strategic adaptive management planning—Restoring a desert ecosystem by managing introduced species and native herbivores and reintroducing mammals. *Conservation Science and Practice, 3*(2). https://doi.org/10.1111/csp2.268

Kirby, P. (2023, July 15). Italy bear attacks: Animals behind Alpine attacks spared slaughter. *BBC News.* https://www.bbc.com/news/world-europe-66198582

Long, S. (2004). Could litigation provide equity where the Kyoto Protocol is failing? *Alternative Law Journal, 29*(2), 92–93. https://doi.org/10.1177 /1037969X0402900207

Boitani, L. & Linnell, J. D. C. (2015). Bringing large mammals back: Large carnivores in Europe. In H. M. Pereira & L. M. Navarro (Eds.), *Rewilding European landscapes* (pp. 67–84). Springer Open. https://doi.org/10.1007/978 -3-319-12039-3

Macdonald, J. (2011). The role of law in adapting to climate change. *WIREs Climate Change*, 2(2), 283–295. https://doi.org/10.1002/wcc.96

Minister for the Environment v. Sharma (2022). FCAFC, 35.

Oposa v. Department of the Environment and Natural Resources (1994), 33 ILM 173.

Pandey, G., & Madhuri, S. (2014). Heavy metals causing toxicity in animals and fishes. *Research Journal of Animal, Veterinary and Fishery Sciences*, 2(2), 17–23.

Peel, J. (2007). The role of climate change litigation in Australia's response to global warming. *Environmental and Planning Law Journal*, 24(2), 90–105.

Peel, J., & Osofsky, H. M. (2018). A rights turn in climate change litigation? *Transnational Environmental Law*, 7(1), 37–67. https://doi.org/10.1017/ S2047102517000292

Perkins, T. (2023, July 24). Lawsuit says US environmental agency ignores harm of biofuel production. *The Guardian*. https://www.theguardian.com/ environment/2023/jul/24/lawsuit-us-epa-biofuel-production-harm

Raustiala, K. (2003). Rethinking the sovereignty debate in international economic law. *Journal of International Economic Law*, 6(4), 841–878. https://doi.org /10.1093/jiel/6.4.841

Rees, J. D., Rees, G. L., Kingsford, R. T., & Letnic, M. (2019). Indirect commensalism between an introduced apex predator and a native avian predator. *Biodiversity and Conservation*, 28(10), 2687–2700. https://doi.org /10.1007/s10531-019-01787-8

Rio declaration on environment and development (1992, June 13), 31 ILM 874.

Ripple, W. J., Wolf, C., Phillips, M. K., Beschta, R. L., Vucetich, J. A., Kauffman, J. B., ... Ashe, D. M. (2022). Rewilding the American West. *BioScience*, 72(10), 931–935. https://doi.org/10.1093/biosci/biac069

Robinson v. Waitakere City Council [2010] NZEnvC 314.

Sharma v. Minister for the Environment [2021] FCA 560.

Stone, C. (1972). Should trees have standing? Towards legal rights for natural objects. *Southern California Law Review*, 45, 459–501.

Stone, C. (2010). *Should trees have standing? Law, morality and the environment* (3rd ed.). Oxford University Press.

Sypnowich, C. (1987). The "withering away" of law. *Studies in Soviet Thought*, 33(4), 305–332.

United Nations. (1992, May 9). *Framework convention on climate change*. 1771 U.N.T.S. 107, 165; S. Treaty Doc No. 102-38 (1992); U.N. Doc. A/AC.237/18 (Part II)/Add.1; 31 I.L.M. 849 (1992)

United Nations. (1992, June 5). *Convention on biological diversity*. 1760 U.N.T.S. 79, 143; 31 I.L.M. 818.

United Nations. (1992, August 12). *Report of the United Nations conference on environment and development*, UN Doc A/CONF.151/26/Rev.1 (Vol.1) ('Rio Declaration')

United Nations. (2023). *Global climate litigation report: 2023 status review*. Nairobi.

Wahi, N. (2022). The evolution of the right to water in India. *Water*, *14*(3), 398. https://doi.org/10.3390/w14030398

Water Act 2007 (Cth).

Zahl-Thanem, A., Burton, R. J. F., Blekesaune, A., Haugen, M. S., & Rønningen, K. (2020). The impact of wolves on psychological distress among farmers in Norway. *Journal of Rural Studies*, *78*, 1–11. https://doi.org/10.1016/j.jrurstud.2020.05.010

Chapter 2

The idea of the legal person

Conceptions of personhood, rights and obligations

Homo vocabulum est naturae; persona juris civilis [Man is a term of nature; person, of civil law]

The term 'personhood' is insufficiently precise to fully frame the implications of legal personhood. The word has complex meanings associated with concepts from science, religion, politics and philosophy. Indeed, it has shifting meanings temporally, between and even within cultures. Intersecting concepts assigning civic rights within a legal framework – concepts like 'citizen' and 'subject' – further complicate the discussion of legal personhood. Similar complexities attach to phrases such as legal person, juristic person, legal entity, natural legal person and artificial legal person. It is necessary to be precise in understanding how these words are being used in advocacy. Naturally, in legal proceedings, relevant terms will be parsed in detail, but where litigation and other forms of advocacy are deployed to bring about social and political change, it is inappropriate to allow words to have a misleading range of meanings. This section will outline the various philosophical approaches and species of personhood in Western domestic legal traditions and the implications of personhood as it attaches to natural and artificial legal persons.

For many laypersons, the term 'person' is synonymous with the term 'human'. 'Persons' are individual humans in being. However, the meanings of 'person' in law are both wider, more defined and more complex – and I use the plural of the word since there are multiple meanings within any one legal system and between legal systems. Not surprisingly, there is a significant mismatch between understandings of the term, which generates uncertainty in communication. This section will attempt to bridge, or at least compare, these multiple meanings with a view to tracing the meanings attributed to personhood in the current movement(s) to extend the concept of personhood to non-human entities. In this

DOI: 10.4324/9781003388272-2

sense, I am undertaking a 'revisionist explication' (Tiedemann, 2020, p. 15) of the concept of personhood to address its inherent vagueness. It is worth noting at the outset that lawyers will generally problematise the word 'person' according to the issue to be resolved. In domestic law (that is, the law of a particular country or state), modern Western jurisdictions typically categorise law as public or private, and remedies and the study and practice of law tend to result in the articulation of rights and duties according to one or the other of these categories. Public lawyers and public international lawyers may use the word 'person' with quite different meanings and implications, and some of these meanings have moral or political, rather than legal, force. Moreover, academic and practising lawyers will have quite different senses of the implications of legal shifts in meaning. Conversely, moral philosophers may pose a conundrum without being interested in the practical implications of legal change.

New trajectories in the meaning of legal personhood work in several legal domains. We can describe these domains in simplified terms as follows:

a. *International law* emanates from international instruments such as United Nations conventions. A longer account of the legal relevance (in domestic law) of international instruments occurs below. The applicability and enforceability of such instruments at domestic level depend on whether the state has acceded to the instrument, whether it has brought the instrument into domestic legislation and whether breach is able to be meaningfully adjudicated and remedied.

b. *International treaties* with binding force on nation-states but of limited applicability to individuals unless a party state has brought the treaty into domestic legislation.

c. *Domestic public law* made up of constitutions, written and unwritten, and other founding documents. Some of these have been developed with an eye to international law, taking meaning from international instruments, whilst others use the same words with older or unrelated meanings, as we will see later in the discussion on 'rights' language.

d. *Domestic public law* derived from common law or legislative oversight of administrative decision-making. In this category, we should place the prerogative writ of *habeas corpus*, traditionally a procedural remedy against officials holding persons prisoner, which has been heavily utilised by advocates for animal personhood.

e. *Domestic private law* in each jurisdiction utilises concepts of personhood in order to organise rules relating to capacity, rights and obligations. The capacity of domestic law to create these obligations arises from the ongoing legitimacy of the state – in democratic regimes, legitimacy is likely to have its source in the political will expressed in periodic elections. This form of legitimacy is administered by a state-maintained system of courts to which people submit either voluntarily or by state force. Critically, the expenditure of public money is also based on the ongoing legitimacy of the state and its instrumentalities but access to public money will often be regulated by public law.

f. *Indigenous or other cultural lore/law* will vary according to the geographic site and may not have a single understanding of personhood or the environment, or even of the separation between persons and their communities or persons and their environment. Traditionally, jurisprudence has drawn a distinction between cultural and legal principles: Thomas (1963, p. 39) notes that '[it] is a commonplace of jurisprudential discussion that one can and must distinguish between customary law, ie, general rules which would be binding without any state activity upon a court, and legal customs, ie, usages which are effective only if and when given force by a court'. He adds the caveat that this distinction should not be drawn too strongly, given that custom may be integrated into the common law 'subject to the court's being satisfied that it is of immemorial observance, reasonable and compatible with the general law' (Thomas, 1963, p. 40). However, as we will see, 'indigenous' understandings of the environment and its relationship with humans often underpin or supplement advocacy for shifts in legal positioning of the environment, either as a whole or in relation to a particular area, giving rise to arguments for forms of legal pluralism. Again, the influence of international law can be seen in the recognition and integration of indigenous law into domestic law.

Domestic private law is the primary source of rights and obligations enforceable against the citizen and between citizens and will derive from case law as a result of judicial proceedings or from legislation. Legal personhood reposing 'human' rights on non-humans at international level is an exertion of moral or normative force, which then falls to be implemented in law at domestic level. Personhood for non-humans from the perspective of private law rights and obligations creates immediate considerations for the superstructure of capitalism, primarily in relation to the range of property, contractual and tortious claims. From the perspective of the Roman division of law into persons, things and actions, this prioritises the 'action', or manner of achieving redress – the legal procedure enabling enforcement of the rights proposed.

The root of the concept of 'person' in the Western tradition of law is often traced to the Roman jurist Gaius (1946–1953). The *Corpus*

Iuris Civilis (made up of the Codex, Digests and Institutes) divided private law into three categories – in *personae, res* and *actiones* (persons, things and legal actions), adopted into England and its colonies through William Blackstone's (1765) *Commentaries* and Edward Coke's (1628–1644) *Institutes*. Similarly, Von Savigny influenced Germanic and other continental jurisdictions (Gaakeer, 2016, p. 289). Roman law categories suffuse modern legal categories and even the content of many legal systems. That the legal concepts are ancient does not necessarily mean that they are irrelevant, but it does mean that they are built upon cultural (including religious) and economic imperatives that may no longer apply. Institutional constraints may no longer be relevant, and the course of judicial precedent may have made aspects of the law redundant, but until an issue arises for determination, the impact of judicial decision-making in each jurisdiction may be unclear. Legal innovation by way of legislation enables more wholesale change, but unless it codifies an area of law, it builds upon the ancient framework of the common law. In other words, concepts such as personhood are situated historically unless changed wholesale by codification.

The etymology of the word 'person' is the *persona* or mask (Esposito, 2012) hiding the personal but facilitating our participation in the public sphere by 'making us a rights-and-duties-bearing person who can effectuate … legal standing' (Gaakeer, 2016). Many, such as German jurist Vultejus, distinguished between the human person and the civil person, with the consequential reasoning that humans (such as slaves) could lack certain civil rights (Kurki, 2017, p. 1073). However, in his 1879 *Lectures on Jurisprudence*, Austin departs from the position of the continental jurists of the time to assert that there is virtually no distinction between the person and the human (meaning that slaves were persons, not things). In terms of more contemporary theorists, Arendt underlines the distinction between the private and the public persona – 'it is a "right-and-duty" bearing person, created by the law, which appears before the law' (Arendt, 1976, pp. 106–107).

Some legal systems have been influenced by competing philosophical approaches; jurists including Grotius, Gottfried Leibniz, Blackstone, Kant, Hegel and Austin maintained the fundamental distinction between the legal status of a thing and the legal status of a person. William Blackstone argued that the 'primary and principal objects of the law are right and wrongs' (Blackstone, 1765, p. 118) and the rights of a person are distinguished from the rights of things – the rights that a person may acquire over objects. It is a feature of more modern jurisprudential discussions to overlay rights – language over personhood so that we see shifts in focus and emphasis arising from modern rights language.

The concept of 'rights' is also contestable and there are multiple ideas about who (or what) can be a repository of rights. John Chipman Gray in his seminal work argues 'the technical legal meaning of a "person" is a subject of legal rights and duties' (Gray, 2019, p. 47). This 'rights holder' view forms the conventional underpinning of many legal systems and demonstrates the importance of 'personhood' as the starting point for the provision of environmental rights. In domestic law, 'rights' language is typically linked to the remedial outcome sought. If there is no right, then there can be no remedy in law, and 'rights' language is finely tuned to the nature of the (legal) wrong and subject to the caveats and exceptions carved out by the common law over centuries of practical application. Conversely, if there is no remedy, there is in practical terms no right. Jurisdictional limits (the limits to the authority and capacity of the court) are therefore relevant since the forum determines the remedy. This is, of course, obviously applicable to geographic jurisdiction, leading to a cascade of consequences for 'rights' language outside jurisdictional limits. This type of 'right' cannot be enforced by someone outside the jurisdiction, for instance. A person in the Sudan cannot seek to enforce a universal human right against the US government, for instance. The remedial options sought can also have resonance with the old causes of action (in the sense of the categories of law upon which an applicant may rely for a remedy). There is no point in seeking to enforce a claim for specific performance of a contract by pleading a case based on the tort of negligence. When a lawyer thinks of a right, therefore, the next thought is often – how is that right to be enforced in a way that repairs the offence?

Widening the classification of persons places pressure on this legal meaning, and Kurki (2017) summarises a range of alternative formulations of the nature of rights. Interest theory formulates rights as the way in which the law protects interests. This perspective does not focus on the repository of rights, but on how rights are protected, and so is more consistent with the enlargement of the group of those in the interests of whom legal protection may be afforded. The 'will' or 'choice' theory again focuses on rights-holding but from the perspective of a person owing duties to another and therefore creating in that person or thing a right. Kurki himself argues that legal personality is a 'cluster concept' incorporating distinct but interconnected incidents.

This brings the language of rights into a contested realm outside but intersecting with law. In its intersection with the law, the language of rights provides a solution to the conundrum set by the detachment of law from the certainty of moral or religious roots. Kennedy notes that 'rights' language can be deployed to bridge the subjectivity of value language and the objectivity of fact language. This, incidentally, curtails the need for the justification of legal norms through democratic or other legitimation mechanisms. He notes that 'rights are mediators between the domain of pure value judgments and the domain of factual judgments' (Kennedy, 2002, p. 184). Using 'rights' reasoning conveys 'universality', and upon acknowledgement of a 'right', it becomes a 'factoid' 'in the sense that "once you acknowledge the existence of the right, then you have to agree that its observance *requires x, y,* and *z*"' (Kennedy, 2002, p. 185).

This point, from the perspective of environmental personhood, is that the language of rights conceals the political aspect of the protections sought and, in some cases, can be used to circumvent legitimate contestation about the use of public funds and other societal resources, as well as priorities between legitimate claims. It may well be that alternative legitimation techniques support the existence of the right – this is clearest in the case of legislation passed by a democratically enacted parliament. Nevertheless, when applying meanings in law, it is necessary to be able to trace the repositories of decision-making. Self-referential reasoning, particularly in legislation, which confuses objective and subjective matters, can undermine fundamental constructs such as the rule of law, but it also speaks to a wider issue in semantic theory. It is not surprising that Lewis Carroll's (1882, p. 124) exchange between Alice and Humpty Dumpty in *Through the Looking Glass* has been frequently cited in case law to describe the issues arising from incautious drafting (*Liversidge v. Anderson* (1942), p. 245 (Lord Atkin); *Minister for Immigration and Multicultural Affairs v. Yusuf* (2001) (Kirby J):

'When *I* use a word', Humpty Dumpty said, in rather a scornful tone, 'it means just what I choose it to mean – neither more nor less'.

'The question is', said Alice, 'whether you *can* make words mean so many different things'.

'The question is', said Humpty Dumpty, 'which is to be master – that's all'.

On one reading, this is a critique of the subjectivist idea that words derive meaning from the intentions of those uttering them; an interesting idea in semantics, but anathema to law, which requires certainty. Uncertainty in legal meaning risks injustice and administrative overreach. Again, it is not possible within the scope of this series to undertake a major review of these philosophical traditions. Moreover, it is unnecessary, other to note the concepts of personhood as signalling a relationship between a thing and certain rights, and the potential distinction between the person as a person and the person as a citizen in the law and subject to the limitations of variable rights in the law. The rights and duties attached to personhood are not immutable; indeed, national legal systems can remove formal recognition of particular persons or classes of persons if it is willing to take the political risk. Conversely, legal personhood can be reposed upon new categories, as in the case of corporations.

Rights language in international law

Despite the centrality of domestic law to the domain of enforceable claims, international law has been asserting increasing normative and practical force on domestic jurisdictions and has a significant bearing on the current narrative on environmental personhood and the 'rights' claims incorporated therein. Amongst the most significant of the international instruments is the Universal Declaration of Human Rights (United Nations, 1948). The concept of international human rights (and the underlying conception of personhood) uses a particular philosophical understanding of rights based on human dignity, a construct that had not, hitherto, been part of all domestic legal systems. Generally, 'human rights' are limited to humans, who are, under the Declaration, 'born in rights'. International human rights are expressions of the obligations owed by states to humans. Human rights under the Declaration are not legal rights as such. Tiedemann (2020, p. 12) describes these rights as 'super-positive', in the sense that they derive from a source of 'higher rank' than the domestic legal system. However, the word 'higher' is problematic if read in the sense that means 'better' or 'more correct', since that relies on an acceptance of universal morality which has not been established. The term 'higher' means that individual legal systems can be evaluated according to whether they sufficiently protect those rights. Evaluation, per se, is not consonant with enforceability in its traditional legal sense. Indeed, the Charter of the United Nations (1945) (which was created by Treaty) explicitly reinforces domestic sovereignty with a non-intervention rule (with the exception of Chapter VII, which deals with measures to be taken in the event of threats to or breaches of the peace and acts of aggression). Nevertheless, the agitation for domestic recognition of rights of nature, and the growing success of that agitation in both common and civil law jurisdictions, demonstrate the influence of international instruments such as the Declaration on domestic law and movement in the idea of sovereignty itself, even in its legal meaning.

The past few decades have seen a shift in the idea of sovereignty to a sense that governments had an 'international licence … granted by the collectivity of states, which … formed the international community' (Taylor, 1999, p. 539). This idea of sovereignty could be considered political, rather than a legal concept; however, the political wields increasing influence over decisions to bring international instruments into domestic law. Moreover, as Taylor (1999) points out, the idea of legal sovereignty of individual states is by no means settled, and the current division between 'internal monopolies of force, taxation and administration' (Taylor, 1999, p. 544) and international law are largely a product of a 'gradual consolidation', at least in Europe, between 1648 and 1815. The devolution of authorities to bodies such as the European Union indicates the malleability of the concept of state competence. Taylor suggests that it is becoming more difficult to reconcile traditional ideas of state sovereignty with the 'compromises ... which resulted from membership of international society' (Taylor, 1999, p. 564). Fassbender (1998) notes that, depending on one's philosophical position, a constitution may have legal, real or ideal effect (Fassbender, 1998, p. 536) and suggests that, in legal terms, the Charter has reached the status of a constitution for the international community.

For lawyers practising in domestic jurisdictions, international law and a close understanding of international instruments will normally be relevant only where interjurisdictional commercial or family disputes are at issue. There are fields in which knowledge of international law is important to an understanding of the jurisdictional limits in the event of a challenge to the validity of legislation. For most lawyers acting in domestic jurisdictions, the domain of international relations would be considered a matter for the executive, and courts demonstrate caution in taking on jurisdiction that would compromise the separation of powers (Schreuer, 1978).

Beyond practitioner perspectives, the attitude towards international instruments and their institutions varies – Western states, for instance, have been said to be 'more open to the external influences that challenge national policy autonomy and more willing to embrace international institutions as a solution' (Raustiala, 2003, p. 878), and Western European states even more so, given their willingness to 'pool' or 'aggregate' sovereignty through the European Union, for instance (Raustiala, 2003, p. 878). What has become normalised in one jurisdiction does not necessarily have the same political force in other jurisdictions, so activists utilising universalising themes will not have the same traction everywhere.

Even for the theorist, the idea of international law depends on perspective:

> Legal theorists fall into roughly three categories. First, general theorists who fit international law into their theories but do so from a position of relative ignorance and non-involvement in foreign affairs ... Secondly, theorists ... who are primarily experts in international law but who propose a theoretical perspective of international law. Finally, there is the small number of *general* theorists who also have substantial expertise in international law.
>
> (Brownlie, 1998, p. 7)

Thus, in communicating ideas of the 'legality' of the positions of sovereign states (or the actions of the citizens of sovereign states) based on international law, we must also make allowances for the malleability of the concept of a legally binding rule. In writing this account, I am taking the conventional practitioner view that international law is premised on the preservation of the sovereignty of individual states, so in the absence of legislative (or, up to a point, case law) specifically enacting laws to give effect to international instruments, they remain non-binding either upon the state or the citizen. However, this view also acknowledges that commentators concede that there is 'no strictly juridical answer to the problem of domestic jurisdiction' (Trindade, 1976, p. 761). For the avoidance of doubt, 'non-binding' here is intended to mean 'non-binding' in domestic law. There are significant economic, strategic, political and other mechanisms that could contribute to a domestic government considering an international instrument to be binding for other reasons (Trachtman, 2010). Thus, a 'right' stated in an international forum (such as the United Nations) is not in itself a right; it is 'one step removed' (Langlois, 2004, p. 244).

All of this is a prelude to the discussion of the main international instruments relied upon to advocate for the legal effectuation of the idea of environmental personhood. These have variously focused on human rights per se (for instance, the Universal Declaration on Human Rights (1948) the United Nations Declaration on the Rights of Persons Belonging to National or Ethnic, Religious and Linguistic Minorities (1992) and the Vienna Declaration and Programme of Action (1993)), environmental sustainability (the Declaration of the United Nations Conference on the Human Environment (Stockholm Declaration) (1972), the World Charter for Nature (1982) and the Rio Declaration on Environment and Development (1992)) and the interaction between environmental and human rights and the adoption of sustainability principles on developing economies (the Declaration on the Right to Development (1986)). The Universal Declaration of the Rights of Mother Earth (2010) and the Incorporation of the Rights of Nature as the organisational focal point in IUCN's decision-making (2012) gave impetus to the campaign to recognise rights of nature at a domestic level. The UN Declaration on the Rights of Indigenous Peoples (2007) has been a critical source for many of the background 'co-management' principles in the constitutional and legislative instruments which have incorporated rights of nature. More recently, the UN recognition that 'the right to a clean, healthy and sustainable environment is a human right' (2022) has provided significant purchase for legal action asserting that failure to comply with environmental sustainability principles is a breach of human rights.

The impact of these and a great number of other instruments is relatively clear where they have been applied at the domestic level. The mechanism by which the instrument is applied is required to ground the rights concepts in a domestic legal infrastructure, including jurisdictional limitations and consequences for breach. They have a less traceable but significant impact on normative value which contributes to the gradual homogenisation of law and culture. Langlois (2004) notes that the

> origins of this high anthropology within the Western intellectual tradition owe much to the historical influence of Christianity ... and to the reinvigoration of rights practice on a global scale after the Second World War. Yet few of today's premier rights theorists would accept the epistemological and ontological claims of Christianity as satisfactory for a contemporary theory of rights, or as a ground for their high anthropology, even as they recognise Christianity's historical influence.
>
> (Langlois, 2004, p. 244)

The problematic ontology of rights language in the abstracted sense of United Nations instruments is a well-known issue, challenging opponents of colonialism with the troubling universality of rights based, at least to a degree, on the cultural mores of dominant Western countries. Khalil (1993) draws attention to this in his analysis of the Vienna Declaration (1993) from the perspective of the distinction between universalism and cultural relativism and notes the challenges posed by the application of individualised rights in different cultural contexts. Rauber (2009) analyses the legitimacy of United Nations instruments and argues that it is based on an unstated Kantian philosophical framework, thereby circumventing philosophical discussion about the legitimacy of law and accepting the proper purpose of the state according to Kantian virtues (such as perpetual peace). Rauber also notes, with Khalil, that Kantian (and therefore UN) logic is not based on experience or empiricism, and 'is neither dependent on nor open to interference by temporal, local, social or cultural contingencies' (Rauber, 2009, p. 51). Also, fundamentally, Rauber notes that 'Kantian practical philosophy departs from a highly plausible premise: the conception of man as a free and autonomous being' (Rauber, 2009, p. 51). Authority in many federated states is premised on human autonomy, and many theories of legitimacy are based on a version of a social contract. The adoption of institutional and legal principles eroding conceptions of legitimacy would again suggest a homogenising tendency. Whilst instruments such as the Declaration on the Rights of Persons Belonging to National or Ethnic, Religious and Linguistic Minorities (1992) and the Declaration on the Rights of Indigenous Peoples (2007) exhort the creation of institutional measures to protect heterogeneity, the underlying conceptual framework tends towards homogeneity in articulating the commonality of accepted rights. The modern concept of rights could be traced through the American Declaration of Independence to the American civil rights movement, the Second Vatican Council and the United Nations' passage of the International Covenant on Civil and Political Rights and the International Covenant on Economic, Social and Cultural Rights (Witte & Latterell, 2015, p. 354). Critics argue that the human rights discourse is 'unidirectional and predictable, a black-and-white construction' derived from a privileged and particular view of the world represented by 'the United Nations, Western states, international non-governmental organizations (INGOs), and senior Western academics' (Mutua, 2001, p. 202).

Persons in law

As foreshadowed, political and philosophical meanings are one thing; legal meanings are quite another, and the legal domain is the primary source of the current level of contestation. Still, *mutata lex non perit*. The strategic use of law by advocates for the environment has as an aim the disruption of legal categories. It is a truism that law is a conservative force, and whilst law can be used to respond to environmental challenges (McDonald, 2011), it is also tritely obvious that law can stand in the way of adaptive responses (in the same sense that *people* stand in the way of adaptive responses). The disruption of traditional legal categories and understandings is an acknowledged component of the activist arsenal. For the reader traversing both realms, the insouciant use of non-legal meanings in legal contexts can be at best a barrier to understanding and at worst a deliberate deception. Part of the issue arises from the democratising effects of social media and the ease of communication across multiple realms; 30 years ago, case law and legislation could be accessed only on paper, commentary occurred only through news media or in academic texts with long lead times and there were multiple gatekeepers in the form of editors, librarians, teachers and academic commentators. Cases were typically argued based on precedents from a single jurisdiction, perhaps drawing upon persuasive precedents from like jurisdictions in novel cases but otherwise keeping close to binding precedents and not stretching analogies. The modern forces for the democratisation of law mean that lawyers can no longer expect to gatekeep concepts such as legal personhood, but that does not mean that the new conceptualisations will withstand legal analysis or even be legally coherent.

Traditional incidents or characteristics of legal personhood include the capacity to sue and to be sued in your own right, the capacity to hold and sell property and the capacity to enter into contracts in your own right. These are rights structured around economic interests and will be reposed in artificial legal persons such as corporations. These rights also attach to most government instrumentalities or authorities which may be corporatised or have certain personhood rights reposed by legislation. Jolly and Menon (2021) noted that legal personhood has been reposed in idols so that endowments made to a deity would remain in the deity's name (*Yogendra Nath Naskar v. Commission of Income-Tax*, Calcutta, 1969). There is no reason, in principle or in law, for personhood to be created in the environment in order to protect the environment or its elements, where protection could be afforded by a government instrumentality. Indeed, in some cases, such as in New Zealand, environmental personhood has been reposed in an area which had been a national park administered by a government instrumentality. The impetus for change arises not because existing mechanisms were not legally capable of protecting the environment, but because there was dissatisfaction with the result. The subtext to the movement for environmental personhood is that the protections sought are against government or administrative decision-making to enable the enforcement of legal rights against the executive. Recall, again, that the creation of an enforcement of rights generally involves decisions about priorities, so this is a process of elevating certain rights-claims against political priorities.

So why would environmental activism focus on personhood as a legal construct? One cogent reason is that, as we have seen, cases seeking legal redress for environmental wrongs have come across problems of legal standing. Legal standing is the capacity to bring an action in court – the 'right to make a legal claim or seek judicial enforcement of a duty or right' (Angstadt, 2016, p. 346). Rules of standing (*locus standi*) traditionally ensured that the litigant bringing proceedings in court has some relevant interest. So, for instance, to bring an action in nuisance, a litigant needed to be a person with some legal interest in the relevant property (such as an owner or lessee). In most jurisdictions, at least traditionally, 'neither trees nor animals have standing' (*Robinson v. Waitakere City Council* 2010, p. 23). Advocacy organisations can also be inhibited by laws of standing from bringing proceedings. For instance, in *Australian Conservation Foundation Inc v. Commonwealth* (1980), a majority of the High Court of Australia held that the Australian Conservation Foundation had no standing to challenge the validity of a decision to approve the development and operation of a resort in Queensland, such a right not having been conferred by the relevant legislation.

The clear answer to the question of standing in cases such as *Australian Conservation Foundation Inc v. Commonwealth* (1980) would be to advocate for change in the legislation. Where the standing rules arise from common law, legislative change could also be pressed. Indeed, standing rules have changed significantly over the years since Stone's (1972) influential article. Advocacy for personhood rights for the environment is not the most direct response. Strategically, the reason for this focus arises from the fact that rules of standing are variable depending on the cause of action and the jurisdiction, but many advocates for the environment work in multiple jurisdictions and seek redress using various causes of action, and part of the arsenal of the advocate is the appeal to successful campaigns in other jurisdictions.

In any event, advocacy for environmental personhood has moved beyond the issue of standing and now seeks a wider range of protections and concepts arising from international, rather than domestic, law. The provision of rights of various forms in the environment or its individual elements has occurred through constitutional reform, legislation and/or court decisions. In legal terms, the incidents of personhood vary substantially. It is, accordingly, dangerous to generalise. However, the recency of legal changes also indicates a liminal element to the current framing of rights. Implementation of legislation has not yet seen results or been subject to challenge by competing rights. Only in Ecuador are we approaching a mature jurisprudence on the issue, and given the fragility of the Ecuadorian state, gains could be swept away. In jurisdictions in which personhood rights are more recent, cases have not yet moved through appeals or been applied with confidence. The trend is likely to accelerate: finalisation of the draft Universal Declaration of River Rights will create further impetus for legislative changes.

Legal personhood of humans

The legal incidents of personhood vary even by reference to human persons. Different legal systems will ascribe different ideas to *in utero*, minor, adult, elderly, imprisoned or unconscious persons. In terms of full engagement in legal transactions and protection, minors and the incapacitated will have very circumscribed legal capacities (for instance, will not be able to hold property, contract in their own right or sue to protect a right). Personal rights can be highly variable in relation to the right to life, autonomy, freedom of movement and protection in particular. Some categories of human rights cut across aspects of civil rights – the civil (state) rights of imprisoned persons, or non-citizens, may be attenuated by reference to the political philosophy and legal framework underlying citizenship in that system. Whilst there is now general agreement in modern states that all categories of humans (regardless of gender, class, occupation and so on) are considered persons, there are still contested categories. Moreover, there is a distinction between human, juridical and civil rights. Even if we take as our starting point the conventional view that a legal person is a rights holder, as a legal definition this is a simplification, and it does not necessarily advance the debate about who or what *should be* a legal person. Different legal systems recognise different persons as having legal personhood. There are some areas in which there is genuine debate arising from deep cultural differences. If we limit the idea of the person to humankind, there remain differences of view about where humanity begins and ends (Raposo et al., 2008). Some communities ascribe legal personhood to the human foetus, zygote or embryo (Kulusika, 2004), for instance, whereas others consider that legal personhood cannot arise until birth, creating concepts such as 'potential person' to describe and delineate arguments for priority in rights (McLean & Petersen, 1996).

There are historical and philosophical bases for the primacy of human interests (over the interests of non-human things) in modern Western legal systems. Some advocates and commentators that concede the real personhood rights of the type sought in theory are incompatible with a post-Enlightenment legal system. Human rights, as progressively identified in international fora and applied domestically, are marked by Enlightenment virtues, drawing upon 'modernity, secularism, progress, technology, liberalism, universalism, and humanitarianism' (Singh, 2010, p. 7), which in application conceals the 'historical reductionism ailing international law's global administrative project' (Singh, 2010, p. 7). Singh points to the 'scientificity' characteristic of post-Enlightenment modernity, and the tendency of international law to advance its own version of colonialism (Singh, 2010, p. 34). In particular, the universality of international law, which is a characteristic of the modern rights agenda, conceals a colonialist view of pre-modernity.

To some degree, modern scholarship advocating the extension of legal rights to the environment often draws upon indigenous legal concepts to support rights-claims. These bases are various; there is no single indigenous ontology, and it is less than helpful to point to indigenous ways of understanding nature and its elements without specifying which peoples, and which nature. Whilst Pecharroman (2018, p. 6) argues that '[t]he paradigm that embraces and understands nature as a being with rights has been part of many indigenous populations' worldviews for hundreds of years', Angstadt and Hourdequin (2021, p. 24) note that this analysis 'operates at a high level of generality and does not explore in detail specific aspects of … compatibilities (as well as potential tensions)'. Hence, the case study technique can demonstrate that the concept is grounded in a particular location. This leaves unresolved questions of temporality and conflicting worldviews, but this will remain unresolved for the purposes of this account (and, perhaps, forever). There also remain open questions about the application of 'scientism' to analyses of indigenous claims and issues of evidence to assess their veracity. The emerging critique of scientism is, in itself, a significant strand in the decolonising agenda and speaks to the underlying issue of discontent with modernity (Coope, 2020).

Artificial legal persons

The concept of the artificial legal person, and the legal capacities afforded such a being, can be instructive for advocates of environmental personhood. Artificial legal persons are created by 'incorporation'. The word 'corporation' is a word derived from the Latin *corpus* or 'body'. The process of 'incorporation' thus is the creation of a new body recognised in law as having some of the characteristics of legal personhood. Sutton's Hospital case (1612) demonstrates the use of the fiction to support charitable purposes. The benefits of the corporate form, which exists in law only, were set out by Sir Edward Coke:

> a Corporation aggregate of many is invisible, immortal, and resteth only in intendment and consideration of the Law; and therefore cannot have predecessor nor successor. They may not commit treason, nor be outlawed, nor excommunicate, for they have no souls, neither can they appear in person, but by Attorney. A Corporation aggregate of many cannot do fealty, for an invisible body cannot be in person, nor can swear, it is not subject to imbecilities, or death of the natural body, and divers other cases.

Legal immortality is also noted as the primary benefit of incorporation in Blackstone's *Commentaries* (Blackstone, 1765, p. 455). The advantage of a corporation over the individual is that personal rights die with the person, but artificial legal persons live in perpetuity.

The clearest modern conceptualisation of the artificial legal person is the private commercial corporation (often called a company), and given the primacy of this form to modern commerce, it has been subject to rigorous legislative, judicial and academic scrutiny. As it is in the interests of commerce to have consistency in corporate forms, corporate structure, limitations and capacities are similar across jurisdictions. This body is, famously, separate from the individuals creating or owning the corporation. This aspect of the modern corporate form was described in the decision of the House of Lords in England in *Salomon v. Salomon & Co Ltd* (1896), and the case remains the primary modern authority to support the conventional view that a commercial corporation has a separate legal personality from its founders and members. In that case, Lord Halsbury LC noted that the *Companies Act* provided the machinery for the creation of the artificial legal person, and therefore recognised that artificial entity. Such an artificial legal person had an existence separate from its shareholders and could enter into contracts on its own behalf, own property, sue and be sued, incur debts, act as agents or trustees and be wound up. The acceptable form and capacities of this legal person were set out in the legislation. The case remains instructive, and indeed is a staple of corporation law curricula; the various arguments for the individual to be liable for the debts of the company leaned heavily on the 'fiction' of legal personality. In argument, the company was described as an 'alias' for its founder and its creation as a 'mere scheme' or fraud. Artificial legal personhood is a common commercial vehicle in the form of the modern company, but the modern company is a successor to more ancient corporate forms acknowledged in Roman law – universities, colleges, municipalities and religious bodies also had corporate forms, and many of these continue to subsist in the form of eleemosynary (charitable) or civil corporations. Many have been updated in form to fall under modern legislation, which is more amenable to modern forms of governance. States can form legal relations with others, for instance (Morss, 2009), but states have legal personhood and foreign states operating within a jurisdiction have legal personhood derived from recognition of the foreign state. In *Law Debenture Trust v. Ukraine* (2023), a foreign state (Ukraine) was held to have the capacity to enter into commercial relations in the UK regardless of limitations in capacity in its own Constitution and domestic law. Instead, it derived legal capacity through recognition of capacity by the executive in the UK.

The corporation, although a legal person, is not able to act on its own. It acts through persons – as Danckwerts J noted in *The Abbey, Malvern v. Ministry of Town & Country Planning* (1951), an artificial legal person 'can only operate by means of human beings ... therefore, one has to see who operates the company ... who, in fact, is in control'. Despite the legal position, the practical position is that there must be persons behind the corporate veil to operate the company. Lord Chancellor Edward Thurlow famously noted that a company has neither 'bodies to be punished, nor souls to be condemned, they therefore do as they like'. Lord Denning reimagined this more pithily in *British Steel Corporation v. Granada Television Ltd* (1980, p. 1127): a corporation 'has no body to be kicked or soul to be damned'. Reaching the natural person behind the corporation – lifting or piercing the corporate veil – is a necessary part of bringing natural legal persons to account for decision-making. This issue has been of a particular moment in the attribution of criminal wrongs to corporations, since typically a *mens rea*, or applicable mental element, must be proven to establish guilt, and corporations have no mind or conscience. More recently, a growing number of strict liability offences have been established, particularly in relation to workplace or occupational safety, to simplify criminal conviction of artificial legal persons, but a parallel legislative movement has criminalised employees or officeholders of corporations to ensure the accountability of persons behind the corporate veil. Incidentally, the strategy of going behind the corporation to its human elements to bring about environmental change has been deployed in many contexts but recent cases have been brought in relation to climate change against fossil fuel companies and those in the food and agriculture sector, transport, plastics and finance (Setzer & Higham, 2022, p. 2).

Legal personhood of non-human animals

The modern movement to recognise legal personhood for non-human animals has followed a sustained philosophical shift. Legal action has not tended to create a firm legal foundation to support legal personhood in animals. Franceschini (2021) relates actions brought on behalf of particular animals, mainly procedural actions such as *habeas corpus* (literally, you – the court – have the body), but also criminal law and copyright. These cases ranged from Brazil in 1972 (relating to caged birds) and 2005, 2008 and 2009 (chimpanzees, criminal procedure and *habeas corpus*), Austria in 2007 (chimpanzee), the United States in 2012 (orcas), Argentina in 2013, 2014 and 2017 (chimpanzees), the United States in 2013 (various actions relating to chimpanzees Tommy, Kiko, Hercules and Leo), Argentina in 2014 (polar bear, orangutan), Argentina in 2015 and 2018 (dogs – involving criminal law), the United States in 2015 (crested black Macaque – a case involving authorship in copyright), the United States in 2017 and 2018 (elephants, *habeas corpus*), Colombia in 2017 (Andean Bear) and India in 2020 (Asian Elephant).

There have, however, been a few successful actions at the time of writing. A 2005 case in Brazil involving the chimpanzee Suiça could be regarded as legally successful since a writ of *habeas corpus* was admitted – even though the animal was poisoned and died before the writ could be concluded. A 2016 Argentinian writ of *habeas corpus* involving a caged chimpanzee, Cecilia, was successful in having Cecilia moved from a poorly designed cage to an animal sanctuary. However, the legal significance of the case can be disputed since the action was settled (Tercer Juzgado de Garantías de Mendoza, 2016). A 2020 case in Pakistan was successful in having a number of animals (elephants, bears and a crocodile) moved from Islamabad's Marghazar Zoo, whilst also setting in place a new management to relocate others.

Most of these cases share the common feature that they were brought in relation to an individual animal or group of named animals, although in legal terms it is also interesting that there have been various legal strategies deployed. *Habeas corpus* writs have dominated, but actions have also been premised on statutes dealing with particular legal categories – criminal law, copyright and animal welfare legislation, for instance. The variation in the definitional terms in statutes between jurisdictions makes the precedential force of these cases quite limited. There are, nevertheless, key insights from this listing. The most obvious point to be made is the growth in the number of cases between 1972 and 2020 and the role of advocacy organisations such as the Great Ape Project, Nonhuman Rights Project, People for the Ethical Treatment of Animals, Free the Wild, Animal Rights Association, Asociación de Funcionarios y Abogados por los Derechos de los Animales (the Association of Public Officials and Attorneys for Animal Rights), Asociación Mendocina de Protección, Ayuda y Refugio del Animal and Amor Animal Paraná (animal protection non-government organisations in Argentina). The choice to utilise legal proceedings instead of (or along with) political, institutional or popular agitation is also interesting. In many of these cases, there were background administrative, financial or logistical considerations which, if not managed, would have made any legal decision moot. Courts are typically unwilling to make an order if it cannot be carried out, or if it would be useless for some other reason. Where the outcome of a judicial proceeding would result in a precedent of such significance, common law courts typically consider the matter to be appropriate for parliament. The choice of animals is also interesting – all but two involved mammals, and most involved primates. The role of the Great Ape Project was, no doubt, significant in the choice of species, but the genetic, behavioural and physical similarities between humans and apes may be strategic in the capacity to increase public sympathy for the animal and therefore the cause. The use of the writ of *habeas corpus*, historically framed for the protection of human beings who are illegally incarcerated, also indicates that the cases are part of a programme of litigation to achieve a certain end and grand aim – recognition that animals have legal personhood. These cases illustrate the role of litigation as both a result of and a prompt to changes in the societal attitude towards animals. Visa Kurki notes that these cases involve activist groups deploying legal and philosophical expertise, but that the strategic use of *habeas corpus* arguments may detract from the eventual goal (Kurki, 2021).

Some cases stand out. In Argentina, in 2019, a case was brought in favour of jaguars as a species. In Uttarakhand, India, in 2018, a case acknowledged 'animals' generally, in relation to animal welfare compliance (Franceschini, 2021, p. 142) and in Haryana, India, the rights of members of the animal kingdom were recognised (Franceschini, 2021, p. 143). The latter two cases align with a more general recognition of the rights of nature, considered in more detail below, and also demonstrate the broader protections argued in some jurisdictions (notably in India and South America).

Legal personhood of artificial intelligence

Modern developments have given rise to further speculation on the nature of personhood. Cultural discourse on the personhood of created beings occurred long before the idea of robots became a practicality. Mary

Shelley's *Frankenstein* (1819) explores themes of humankind usurping God, responsibility for created life and a number of Enlightenment themes such as the dominance of reason over superstition and the separation of church and state. The work of Isaac Asimov, the significant impact of movies such as *2001: A Space Odyssey* (1968), *Blade Runner* (1982) and *I, Robot* (2004) and a now significant number of inter-cultural referents demonstrate the durable interest in these themes. The dystopian elements of many of these referents (see, for instance, the *Terminator* series) and a parallel interrogation of themes of responsibility for our own creations – and mistakes – speak to an ongoing fascination with the nature of being. Nevertheless, the recent legal commentary on robot personhood has not typically, as in the case of animals or the environment, been a discourse on the creation or recognition of protective rights for artificial beings (with some exceptions – Peter Singer has argued that when robots become conscious, they should have rights) (Weber, 2023). Cases to date have denied copyright protection to artificial intelligence – in *Thaler v. Perlmutter* (2023), the plaintiff, Thaler, owned a computer which 'generated a piece of visual art of its own accord'. Thaler sought to have the copyright registered with the machine listed as the author, claiming that as the owner of the machine, the copyright should then be transferred to him. This was refused on the grounds that a human author must be nominated.

In the case of artificial intelligence, commentators typically have argued that personhood is a device to enable the attribution of legal responsibility to damage caused by artificial beings. This is particularly significant in the case of artificial intelligence capable of responding to external stimuli and thus capable of damaging others without intervening human action (Bertolini & Aiello, 2018, p. 131). This has moved beyond speculation. Recommendations of the European Parliament in 2017 were framed in terms of a requirement that there be human control over intelligent machines (Bertolini & Aiello, 2018, p. 131). The purpose of proposed registration is to repose liability for robot action to a human and to require human control over machines in much the same way as corporate responsibility can be allocated to a human with governance duties. Other analogies arise for autonomous vehicles, the ubiquity of which requires immediate legal consideration. King, for instance, suggests that liability for autonomous vehicles should be ascribed on the same basis as applies to a horse being used for transport purposes (King, 2018). There have been reports of interactive artificial intelligence encouraging interlocutors to take their own lives (Cost, 2023), or people finding themselves defamed by materials created by ChatGPT (Kaye, 2023), increasing the pressure to assign liability to a legal person, preferably one with assets to satisfy judgement – to pay any compensation ordered by the court.

Collectives, commons and interactive organisms

Collectives – groups of people or things – do not typically have legal rights per se. A collective is not a thing, and the capacity of collectives and interactive organisms to be 'persons' is, on the face of it, also highly counterintuitive. 'Personhood' typically refers to an independent unitary body. Where groups of persons act together as 'unincorporated associations', the association is not recognised as an independent entity in legal terms and legal actions such as holding property, contracting, suing or being sued occur through the human agents. Where a group seeks to assert a right, it is ordinarily done through a public agency. For instance, where emissions from a property affect the amenity of a number of surrounding landowners, an action in public nuisance will be taken by the attorney general on behalf of those persons.

The premise that rights subsist in non-incorporated collectives raises a range of legal questions, but one of the main issues is the trend towards legal pluralism underlying the claim for collective rights. Rights to self-government of collectives, particularly indigenous groupings, are a strong theme in contemporary legal literature and are theorised to form the normative basis for resource rights (Nine, 2013). The idea of the personhood of a collective, particularly one which is undefined and with shifting membership, is problematic in law and yet is a central issue in recognising the personhood of the environment. The interactivity of an ecosystem is essential to its continued functioning, so the argument is that the recognition of the personhood of an ecosystem as such is necessary for its protection. This, broadly, motivates recognition of other collectives, such as coral reefs, river systems, aquifers, wetlands and similarly interactive environmental elements.

Contemporary cultural references to the being and rights of collectives are not uncommon and are often linked to indigenous ontologies, once more raising issues of implementation of the United Nations Declaration on the Rights of Indigenous Peoples (2007). Thus, it is sometimes argued that artistic representations of indigenous knowledge are cultural assets owned by a particular group, raising issues for ownership of intellectual property (Carpenter, 2004; Oruç, 2022). Indeed, traditional intellectual property law is ill-adapted to provide a framework for acknowledging community authorship of indigenous heritage, given that the goal of intellectual property is typically to mediate the societal good in promulgating the work and the rights of the author to be recompensed and acknowledged, whereas the community might very well be seeking to keep the work within a privileged group. Oruç (2022, p. 251) notes that

> [it] is widely argued in the literature that intellectual property law at its core is incompatible with Indigenous heritage. The underlying

reason is that systems like copyright focus too much on the knowledge's engagement with the market, therefore insisting that having the Indigenous communities embrace copyright could amount to forcing the community to adjust to something outside their belief system.

For present purposes, it is sufficient to note that the law typically prefers to deal with a person, not an unincorporated collective, and where indigenous rights to collective knowledge have been acknowledged, it may not enable the transactional elements required to exploit traditional knowledge for commercial gain. To do this requires legislative change to ensure the type of protection sought.

In the case of ecosystems, the issue of collectivity is even more complex. In Stone's (2010) analysis, one of the key arguments supporting legal standing is to enable damage to the environment to be remedied in its own right, rather than seeking a remedy on the basis that injury was caused to a human person as a result of damage to the environment. Identifying the 'wronged person' by isolating the environmental element, with or without interacting systems and organisms, would be far more legally complex than the 'unascertained class', which typically bespeaks unforeseeability in the tort of negligence (and bars recovery) and triggers the suspension of vesting in the law of succession. It would also be more complex than the idea of uncertainty, which is fatal to contractual validity. The common law craves certainty, as indeed, generally, do people when it comes to matters upon which they can sue or be sued.

Legal personhood of the environment

As we have seen, personhood has long been extended to non-human entities – corporations are artificial legal persons and held at law to have certain legal rights and duties that would otherwise only be exercisable by human persons. The exigencies recognised by private law have meant that the term personhood is absolutely capable of taking in non-human forms. However, the legal definition of personhood has not traditionally moved beyond the recognition of corporations (in their various forms) as holders of confined legal characteristics normally ascribed to natural legal persons. Since the idea of personhood engages cultural, moral, scientific and religious views, there is scope for narrative fluidity in the use of the term, however, in most current legal conceptualisations of the person, there is general agreement that animals, plants, trees, rivers and other non-human elements of nature are not persons. They are, instead, 'things', which may be held as real or personal property. As things, they cannot themselves hold rights, and persons may have rights over them.

Challenges to this idea have been increasing. Whilst some analyses and legal approaches have focused on non-human animals as persons, there has been a steady trickle of case law and legislation acknowledging some of the legal attributes of personhood to other aspects of nature. Several countries have now held that nature, or parts of nature, have juristic personhood in some form. The repositories of personhood have extended beyond animals to rivers, lakes, highlands, jungles, forests, glaciers, ecosystems and Mother Earth or nature itself. The consequences of personhood in each case vary, having arisen from judicial decision-making, legislation or Constitutional provision across disparate legal contexts.

In the case of legislation relating to particular and limited ecosystems, this has been lauded as an entirely novel step with the potential to fundamentally reframe the law and avenues for the protection of ecosystems. This is typically an overreaction. For instance, rights for nature have been granted or acknowledged in New Zealand (the Whanganui River), Canada (the Muteshekau-shipu/Magpie River), Australia (the Yarra River), Ecuador (the Vilcabamba River and Pachamama/Mother Earth), Uganda ('Nature'), Bolivia (Pachamama/Mother Earth), Panama and Spain (the Mar Menor Lagoon). However, these do not necessarily confer personhood rights (some acknowledge a 'living entity'). In other cases, such as in the case of the Indian Ganges and Yamuna Rivers and the Atrato, Magdalena, Cauca, Río de la Plata, Coello, Combeima, Cocora and Otún in Columbia (Wesche, 2021), state courts have conferred legal personhood. In some cases, the claims have been contested on appeal and the parameters of the stated personhood remain unclear.

Other cases in which fundamental constitutional changes or case law in superior courts have reposed personhood or a suite of rights approaching personhood in the environment raise important questions such as the priority of legal rights and the conferral of ancillary obligations on non-human persons. In essence, the creation of these new forms of personhood makes a powerful statement of the inherent value of nature *apart from* ecosystem value to humans. It thus tends to challenge the anthropocentric ideation of human law as in service to humans and to conceptualise humans as only part of an integrated system – and not necessarily the most important part. Some advocates argue that 'nature's rights come first, followed by human rights and then corporate rights' (Barkham, 2021). Some commentators suggest that 'we seem to be witnessing something important. What we increasingly observe in social media is the anthropomorphising of nature, personification of trees, humanization of animals and animization of men' (Gwiazdowicz et al., 2022). In Chapter 3, we will consider in several case studies different versions of legal personhood in nature, or its elements, and the constitutional and/or legislative infrastructure, or, in some cases, judicial decision-making that has given the concept legally binding force.

References

Abbey Malvern Wells Ltd v. Ministry of Local Government and Planning [1951] Ch 728.

Angstadt, J. M. (2016). Securing access to justice through environmental courts and tribunals: A case in diversity. *Vermont Journal of Environmental Law*, *17*, 345–371.

Angstadt, J. M., & Marion, H. (2021). Taking stock of the rights of nature. In D. P. Corrigan & M. Oksanen (Eds.), *Rights of nature - a re-examination* (pp. 14–35). Routledge.

Arendt, H. (1976). *On revolution*. Penguin.

Austin, J. (1879). *Lectures on jurisprudence* (Vol. 2). John Murray.

Australian Conservation Foundation Inc v. Commonwealth (1980) 146 CLR 493.

Barkham, P. (2021, July 25). Should rivers have the same rights as people? *The Guardian*. Retrieved May 19, 2023, from https://www.theguardian.com/environment/2021/jul/25/rivers-around-the-world-rivers-are-gaining-the-same-legal-rights-as-people

Bertolini, A., & Aiello, G. (2018). Robot companions: A legal and ethical analysis. *Information Society*, *34*(3), 130–140. https://doi.org/10.1080/01972243.2018.1444249

Blackstone, W. (1765). *Commentaries on the laws of England in four books*. Clarendon Press. https://www.gutenberg.org/files/30802/30802-h/30802-h.htm

British Steel Corporation v. Granada Television Ltd [1980] 3 WLR 774 (HG); 797 (CA); 818 (HL).

Brownlie, I. (1998). *The rule of law in international affairs*. Kluwer Law International.

Carpenter, M. M. (2004). Intellectual property law and indigenous peoples: Adapting copyright law to the needs of a global community. *Yale Human Rights and Development Law Journal*, *7*, 51–78.

Carroll, L. (1882). *Through the looking glass, and what Alice Found there*. Macmillan.

Coke, E. (1628–1644). *Institutes of the Lawes of England*.

Coope, J. (2020). Indigenous knowledge and techno-scientific modernity: "hierarchical integration" reconsidered. *Ecologicalpsychology*, *12*(2), 151–157.

Cost, B. (2023, March 30). Married father commits suicide after encouragement by AI chatbot: Widow. *New York Post*. https://nypost.com/2023/03/30/married-father-commits-suicide-after-encouragement-by-ai-chatbot-widow/

Esposito, R. (2012). The dispositif of the person. *Law, Culture and the Humanities*, *8*(1), 17–30. https://doi.org/10.1177/1743872111403104

Fassbender, B. (1998). The United Nations Charter as constitution of the international community. *Columbia Journal of Transnational Law*, *36*(3), 529.

Franceschini, M. M. (2021). Animal personhood: The quest for recognition. *Animal & Natural Resource Law Review, 17*, 93–150.

Gaakeer, J. (2016). "Sua cuique persona?" A note on the fiction of legal personhood and a reflection on interdisciplinary consequences. *Law and Literature, 28*(3), 287–317. https://doi.org/10.1080/1535685X.2016.1232920

Gaius. (1946–1953). *Institutiones.* Clarendon Press.

Gray, J. C. (2019). *The nature and sources of the law.* Routledge.

Gwiazdowicz, D. J., Matulewska, A. E., & Piskorski, J. (2022). The ban on participation of children and teenagers in the hunt in Poland – A case study of parliamentary law enactment process and its consequences. *International Journal for the Semiotics of Law, 36*(2), 939–968. https://doi.org/10.1007/s11196-022-09934-1

IUCN. (2012). Incorporation of the Rights of Nature as the organizational focal point in IUCN's decision making' Resolution WCC-2012-Res-100-EN. https://portals.iucn.org/library/node/44067

Jolly, S., & Menon, K. (2021). Of ebbs and flows: Understanding the legal consequences of granting personhood to natural entities in India. *Transnational Environmental Law, 10*(3), 467–492. https://doi.org/10.1017/S2047102520000424

Kaye, B. (2023, April 6). Australian mayor readies world's first defamation lawsuit over ChatGPT content. Reuters. https://www.reuters.com/technology/australian-mayor-readies-worlds-first-defamation-lawsuit-over-chatgpt-content-2023-04-05/

Kennedy, D. (2002). The critique of rights in critical legal studies. In W. Brown & J. Halley (Eds.), *Left legalism/left critique.* Duke University Press.

Khalil, N. M. (1993). Paragraph 3, Part II of the Vienna Declaration and Programme of Action 1993: A reflection of the approach of the universalist or the cultural relativist? *Journal of Malaysian and Comparative Law, 20*, 183–202. https://ejournal.um.edu.my/index.php/JMCL/article/view/16083

King, D. (2018). Putting the reins on autonomous vehicle liability: Why horse accidents are the best common law analogy. *North Carolina Journal of Law and Technology, 19*(4), 127–159. https://scholarship.law.unc.edu/ncjolt/vol19/iss4/5

Kulusika, S. E. (2004). The rights of the foetus: An overview. *Zambia Law Journal, 36*, 111.

Kurki, V. (2017). Animals, slaves, and corporations: Analyzing legal thinghood. *German Law Journal, 18*(5), 1069–1090. https://doi.org/10.1017/S2071832200022252

Kurki, V. (2021). Legal personhood and animal rights. *Journal of Animal Ethics, 11*(1), 47–62.

Langlois, A. J. (2004). The elusive ontology of human rights. *Global Society, 18*(3), 243–261. https://doi.org/10.1080/1360082042000221469

Law Debenture Trust v. Ukraine [2023] UKSC 11.

Liversidge v. Anderson [1942] AC 206.

McDonald, J. (2011). The role of law in adapting to climate change. *WIREs Climate Change, 2*(2), 283. https://doi.org/10.1002/wcc.96

McLean, S. A. M., & Petersen, K. (1996). Patient status: The foetus and the pregnant woman. *Australian Journal of Human Rights, 2*(2), 229–241. https://doi.org/10.1080/1323238X.1996.11910957

Minister for Immigration and Multicultural Affairs v. Yusuf (2001) 206 CLR 323.

Morss, J. (2009). The legal relations of collectives: Belated insights from Hohfeld. *Leiden Journal of International Law, 22*(2), 289–305. https://doi.org/10.1017 /S0922156509005822

Mutua, M. (2001). Savages, victims, and saviors: The metaphor of human rights. *Harvard International Law Journal, 42*(1), 201.

Nine, C. (2013). Resource rights. *Political Studies, 61*(2), 232–249.

Oruç, P. (2022). Documenting Indigenous oral traditions: Copyright for control. *International Journal of Cultural Property, 29*(3), 243–264.

Pecharroman, L. C. (2018). Rights of nature: Rivers that can stand in court. *Resources, 7*(13), 23–36. https://doi.org/10.3390/resources7010013

Raposo, V. L., Prata, C., & Ortigão de Oliveira, I. (2008). Human rights in today's ethics: Human rights of the unborn (embryos and foetus)? *Cuadernos Constitucionales de la Cátedra Fadrique Furió Ceriol, 62,* 95–111.

Rauber, J. (2009). The United Nations – A Kantian dream come true – Philosophical perspectives on the constitutional legitimacy of the world organisation. *Hanse Law Review, 5*(1), 49.

Raustiala, K. (2003). Rethinking the sovereignty debate in international economic law. *Journal of International Economic Law, 6*(4), 841–878.

Robinson v. Waitakere City Council [2010] NZEnvC 314.

Salomon v. Salomon & Co Ltd (1896) AC 22.

Schreuer, C. H. (1978). The relevance of United Nations decisions in domestic litigation. *International and Comparative Law Quarterly, 27*(1), 1–17. https:// doi.org/10.1093/iclqaj/27.1.1

Setzer, J., & Higham, C. (2022). *Global trends in climate change litigation: 2022 snapshot.* Grantham Research Institute on climate change and the environment and Centre for Climate Change Economics and Policy. London School of Economics and Political Science.

Shelley, M. (1819). *Frankenstein; or the modern Prometheus.* Routledge.

Singh, P. (2010). The scandal of enlightenment and the birth of disciplines: Is international law a science? *International Community Law Review, 12*(1), 5–34. https://doi.org/10.1163/187197410X12631788215792

Stone, C. (1972). Should trees have standing? Towards legal rights for natural objects. *Southern California Law Review, 45,* 459–501.

Stone, C. (2010). *Should trees have standing? Law, morality and the environment* (3rd ed.). Oxford University Press.

Sutton's Hospital case (1612) 77 Eng Rep 960.

Taylor, P. (1999). The United Nations in the 1990s: Proactive cosmopolitanism and the issue of sovereignty. *Political Studies, XLVII,* 538–565.

Tercer juzgado de garantías de Mendoza [J.G.Men.] [Third Criminal Court of Mendoza], 3/11/2016, "Presentación Efectuada Por AFADA Respecto del Chimpancé 'Cecilia' Sujeto No Humano" [Expte. Nro.] P-72.254/15, (Arg.) "Presentation Made by AFADA Regarding the Chimpanzee 'Cecilia' Non-Human Subject" [File. No.] P-72.254/15, (Arg.).

Thaler v. Perlmutter (2023). District of Columbia, Civil Action No. 22-1564 (BAH) 18 August 2023 (Judge Beryl A Howell). https://scholar.google.com.au /scholar_case?case=7589804851389883065.

Thomas, J. A. C. (1963). Custom and Roman law. *Tijdschrift voor Rechtsgeschiedenis/Legal History Review*, *31*(1), 39.

Tiedemann, P. (2020). *Philosophical foundation of human rights*. Springer Nature.

Trachtman, J. P. (2010). International law and domestic political coalitions: The grand theory of compliance with international law. *Chicago Journal of International Law*, *11*(1), 127.

Trindade, A. (1976). The domestic jurisdiction of states in the practice of the United Nations and regional organisations. *International and Comparative Law Quarterly*, *25*(4), 715–765. https://doi.org/10.1093/iclqaj/25.4.715

United Nations. (1945). Charter of the United Nations, 24 October, 1 UNTS, XVI.

United Nations. (1948). Universal declaration of human rights, GA Res 217A (III), UN GAOR, UN Doc A/810 (10 December).

United Nations. (1992). Report of the United Nations conference on environment and development, UN Doc A/CONF.151/26/Rev.1 (Vol.1) (August 12) ('Rio Declaration').

United Nations. (1992). Declaration on the rights of persons belonging to national or ethnic, religious and linguistic minorities. GA Res 47/135, UN GAOR, 47th sess, 92nd plen mtg, Supp No 49, UN Doc A/47/49 (18 December).

United Nations. (2007). Declaration on the rights of Indigenous peoples, GA Res 61/295, UN Doc A/RES/61/295 (2 October, adopted 13 September 2007).

United Nations General Assembly. (1972). United Nations conference on the human environment. 15 December 1972, A/RES/2994 ('Stockholm Declaration').

United Nations General Assembly. (1982). *The world charter for nature*. United Nations General Assembly.

United Nations General Assembly. (1986). Declaration on the right to development, G.A. Res 41/120.

United Nations General Assembly. (1993). Vienna declaration and programme of action' world conference on human rights (Vienna 14–25 June 1993) (25 June 1993) UN Doc A/CONF.157/23.

United Nations General Assembly. (2022). Declaration on the human right to a clean, healthy and sustainable environment. GA Res 217A (III), UN GAOR, UN Doc A/810 (10 December).

Weber, D. (2023, May 8). Philosopher Peter Singer weighs in on AI, robot rights and being kinder to animals. *ABC News*. Retrieved June 7, 2023, from https://www.abc.net.au/news/2023-05-08/peter-singer-on-ai-robot-rights/102303010.

Wesche, P. (2021). Rights of nature in practice: A case study on the impacts of the Colombian Atrato River decision. *Journal of Environmental Law*, *33*(3), 531–555.

Witte, J. Jr., & Latterell, J. J. (2015). Christianity and human rights: Past contributions and future challenges. *Journal of Law and Religion*, *30*(3), 353–385.

Yogendra Nath Naskar v. Commission of Income-Tax, Calcutta (1969) SCR (3) 742.

Chapter 3

Case studies

Modern incidents of environmental personhood

This then is the general signification of law, a rule of action dictated by some superior being; and in those creatures that have neither the power to think, nor to will, such laws must be invariably obeyed, so long as the creature itself subsists, for its existence depends on that obedience. But laws, in their more confined sense, and in which it is our present business to consider them, denote the rules, not of action in general, but of human action or conduct: that is, the precepts by which man, the noblest of all sublunary beings, a creature endowed with both reason and freewill, is commanded to make use of those faculties in the general regulation of his behavior.
[Blackstone]

Pacha Mama (Ecuador)

Ecuador was the first country to afford specific constitutional acknowledgement of environmental personhood. Ecuador is a country in South America, bordered by the South Pacific Ocean, Colombia and Peru, and including parts of the Amazon jungle and the ecologically significant Galápagos Islands. It was colonised by Spain but obtained independence in 1830. It has had 20 constitutional iterations at the time of writing; the original 1830 Constitution, followed by several further iterations in the 1800s with varying forms of citizen suffrage. During the 1900s, a series of crises prompted further constitutions, interrupted by military coups d'état. Points of contention included the representation of Indigenous peoples, the role of the Roman Catholic Church and the applicability of colonial parliamentary structures, backgrounding current issues relating to colonialism, pluralism and secularism. The 2008 Constitution was designed over several years in the context of discontent over indigenous interests, participatory democracy and 'neo-liberal policies that had shifted wealth from marginalized peoples to elite corporate interests' (Becker, 2011, p. 47). The convocation of a constituent assembly was intended to disrupt the oligarchical control of politics and the economy and ushered in a broadly leftist social and economic agenda.

DOI: 10.4324/9781003388272-3

Pacha Mama (Mother Earth) was recognised in a 2008 amendment to the Constitution (Constitucion de la Republica del Ecuador Ch VII Art 71, Art 72) as an entity with legal rights. The amendment has been described as conceptualising

> the idea of *buen vivir* or 'good living' – living in harmony with Nature as its own entity ... epitomized by both the *quichua* expression *sumak kawsay*, and the *aymara* term *suma qamaña* ... [as part of] a larger and alternative proposal to global capitalism.
>
> (Berros, 2017, p. 37)

The 'good way of living, the sumak kawsa' is recognised in the preamble to the Constitution and the 'Rights of the Good Way of Living' are set out in Chapter 2 Section 1, particularly Art 14. The provisions thus acknowledge people and the environment as different but intertwined in interest.

The Ecuadorean approach has been echoed by other Central American jurisdictions. Article 32 of the Bolivian Constitution gives persons the right, by themselves or in a collective, to take action to defend the rights of the environment, without the usual standing requirement of personal harm. In this way, the Bolivian Constitution could avoid the problem of judicial standing without reposing rights in the environment. Nevertheless, in *Ley de Derechos de la Madre Tierra* [Law of the Rights of Mother Earth] (Bol) (2010), Ch II Art 3, Ch I Art 2, and subsequent regulations (*Universal Declaration of the Rights of Mother Earth*, 2010, Bolivia; *Framework Act on Mother Earth and Holistic Development to Live Well*, 2012, Bolivia). Bolivia legislatively provided for the rights of nature by reposing legal rights to life, freedom from pollution and restoration in Madre Tierra (Mother Earth). An ombudsman was created by Article 10 with oversight obligations (Chaturvedi, 2019, p. 720). In Colombia, the Supreme Court heard a 'climate change' case brought by a group of children challenging deforestation in the Amazon region which, they said, compromised their 'right to a healthy environment, life, health, and the rights of future generations' (Delgado, 2022, pp. 4–5). Delgado reports that '[t]he Court concluded that to protect the environment and ensure the fulfilment of Colombia's climate change obligations, the Colombian Amazon Region was to be entitled to certain rights: the right to protection, conservation, maintenance, and reparation' (Delgado, 2022, p. 5).

Ecuador is considered a 'developing' economy. This is significant because the imposition of international pressure to conform to environmental standards such as emission reduction, land-clearing and pollution remediation can have a greater impact on developing economies, which have not had the opportunity to benefit economically from their natural resources that have enriched developed countries. This is a well-known complexity in the pursuit of environmental goals globally – it could be argued that by requiring the environmental standards of developed economies, developing economies are 'locked into' their current state of development in a way that could disproportionately affect already disadvantaged Indigenous peoples. The United Nations Conference on the Human Environment in Stockholm in 1972 was almost stymied by the reluctance of developing nations to accede to measures that would diminish their capacity to exploit their own resources (Head, 1978, p. 270). The conference created the United Nations Environment Programme and an Action Plan that had as part of the framework financial aid to developing nations. The World Commission on Environment and Development's report *Our Common Future* (1987), in which sustainable development grounded the goals of a 'more prosperous, more just, and more secure' future, acknowledged that 'it is impossible to separate economic development issues from environment issues' (at para 8) and that there is a link between poverty and environmental problems. Constraints on resource extraction and utilisation also have an impact at the level of the individual enterprise or family, as they are also disproportionately affected by laws preventing them from utilising the environment. Thus, 'development' of the economy is built into the idea of 'sustainable development' both as a way of ameliorating injustice and the growing gap between rich and poor countries, and to elicit the agreement of developing nations to the strategies. The use of carbon sequestration programmes in Ecuador to 'pay' people to maintain the environment is one method of overcoming this issue, but with contestable results from the perspective of resolving the issue of distributive justice (McBurney et al., 2022). Conversely, from the perspective of addressing global environmental catastrophe, the concept of sustainable development has reinforced, for some, the need for fundamental institutional change.

The Constitution of Ecuador Art 1 establishes it as a 'constitutional State of rights and justice, a social, democratic, sovereign, independent, unitary, intercultural, multinational and secular State … organized as a republic and governed using a decentralized approach'. It vests sovereignty with 'the people, whose will is the basis of all authority', to be exercised through public bodies. Article 71 states that 'Nature, or Pacha Mama, where life is reproduced and occurs, has the right to integral respect for its existence and for the maintenance and regeneration of its life cycles, structure, functions and evolutionary processes'. Art 72 creates (or acknowledges) nature's right to restoration *in its own right* and apart from the rights of people or corporations in the environment to be restored. The Constitution thus grants positive rights to respect and restoration. These rights are in addition to the separate obligation of people and communities dependent on ecosystems to be compensated in the event of the use of environmental elements or damage to the environment. The State is required to establish mechanisms to restore the environment in the event of a severe or permanent impact and to adopt measures to eliminate or mitigate negative environmental impacts. However, the State's prime duties, set out in Article 3, cl 5, include '[p]lanning national development, eliminating poverty, and promoting sustainable development and the equitable redistribution of resources and wealth to enable access to the good way of living'.

The Constitution lists persons who are Ecuadorian (by birth or naturalisation) and these 'persons, communities, peoples, nations and communities' are *bearers* of rights, and shall enjoy the rights guaranteed to them in the Constitution and in international instruments. Thus, the widest set of constitutional rights are reposed in those persons (Art 10). Nature, by contrast, 'shall be the *subject* of those rights that the Constitution recognizes for it' (Art 10). These concepts raise significant questions for constitutional interpretation – what is the distinction between 'bearers' of rights and 'the subject' of rights, and who has the role of enforcement in each case? Does nature participate in the Constitution guarantees set out in Art 11, that 'all principles and rights are unalienable, obligatory, indivisible, interdependent and of equal importance'? In other words, does the right of nature to existence, maintenance and regeneration have equal importance with the human right to water and food? Clearly, this is not the intention of the provision, since Art 12 refers to a human right to water that cannot be waived, and Art 13 confers on (human) persons the 'right to safe and permanent access to healthy, sufficient and nutritional food, preferably produced locally and in keeping with their various identities and cultural traditions'.

The central thrust of the protection seems to be the cluster of priorities set out in Art 14, which recognises 'the right of the population to live in a healthy and ecologically balanced environment that guarantees sustainability and the good way of living (sumak kawsay)'. By contrast, 'environmental conservation, the protection of ecosystems, biodiversity and the integrity of the country's genetic assets, the prevention of environmental damage, and the recovery of degraded natural spaces are declared matters of public interest'. Accordingly, the Constitution appears to recognise priority for humans in the environment, but development of the environment to achieve the range of human rights must be achieved in a way that preserves the environment – partly, again, for the future benefit of human persons and communities. This falls short of the ecocentric approach sought by many activists. Indeed, the inherent tension between the rights of human persons and communities and the rights of the environment was apparent immediately after the constitutional provisions were enacted when the President sought to expand mining and oil extraction. Kauffman and Martin (2017) report that the President contended that mining practices could be carried out in a socially and environmentally responsible manner and that this could be ensured by the state. 'Moreover, profits from mining and oil extraction were necessary to develop a post-fossil fuel energy sector, reduce poverty, and expand access to education, healthcare, and other public goods. For Ecuador's government, these goals constituted buen vivir' (Kauffman & Martin, 2017, p. 132).

This uneasy tension between the development rights of human persons and the inherent rights of the environment is echoed in the collective rights of indigenous communities and peoples. Article 57 lists several collective rights, said to be 'in conformity with the Constitution and human rights instruments', and these include ownership of community lands (Art 57 cl 4), ownership of ancestral lands (Art 57 cl 5) and participation in the 'use, usufruct, administration and conservation of natural renewable resources located on their lands' (Art 57 cl 6). Allowing for variations in the legal meaning of property, the ownership, use and extraction of ecosystem elements is clearly anticipated, even in the case of non-renewable resources, as long as 'free prior informed consultation' has taken place: Art 57 cl 7. This does not apply to 'the territories of the peoples living in voluntary isolation'. Extractive activities are forbidden in those territories. In other words, the provisions establish contests between norms, requiring attributions of relative value. They require a suite of legislation to clothe the norms in the detail required for justiciability and the creation of institutions to interpret the provisions. Kauffman and Martin (2017), however, note that there has been no political will to establish the legislation necessary to implement the rights of nature as expressed in the constitutional provisions. This is certainly partially an expression of the tensions inherent in the concept of 'sustainable development' in the context of developing economies. Indeed, the approval of mineral extraction without prior consultation by President Rafael Correa in 2009 on the basis that it would create new jobs pointed to the weakness of a constitutional safeguard (Becker, 2011, p. 58).

In the absence of clear legislative provisions, activists engaged in strategic litigation to create the precedents that would help to clothe the constitutional provisions. Article 71 guarantees access to the courts – individuals, groups and communities can take legal action on behalf of 'nature'. The constitutional amendment has been the subject of judicial interpretation by the Constitutional Court of Ecuador. These decisions have given shape to some of the wider questions arising from the designation of nature as a subject of rights. In *Wheeler v. Director de la*

Procuraduria General del Estado en Loja, Corte Provincial de Justicia de Loja (2011), a road expansion project was commenced without an environmental impact assessment, resulting in the diversion of the Vilcabamba River. The petitioners sought to stop the development and based their argument on the rights of the river to its natural course. The petitioners were successful, and the court held that the provincial government had violated the rights of nature. The court noted that the Constitution

> without precedent in the history of humanity, recognizes nature as a subject of rights. Article 71 affirms that: Nature, or Pachamama, where life is reproduced and occurs, has the right to integral respect for its existence and for the maintenance and regeneration of its life cycles, structure, functions, and evolutionary processes.
>
> (*Wheeler v. Director de la Procuraduria General del Estado en Loja, Corte Provincial de Justicia de Loja*, 2011)

A number of cases have cited the constitutional provisions since *Wheeler* and claims for the rights of nature have had varying success. Kauffman and Martin (2017) note that cases brought by the State have been successful against illegal mining, prosecuted hunters and removed shrimp farmers from reserves (Kauffman & Martin, 2017, p. 137). Many of these cases are characterised by the difficulty in establishing the priority of claims for constitutional rights to property, work and other obligations under Article 3, cl 5 of the Constitution, and the lack of common meaning inherent in the underlying concepts contributes to the difficulty in resolving claims. Kauffman and Martin (2017) note that 'Ecuador's RoN [rights of nature] provisions resulted from the activism of a diverse array of indigenous, environmental, and leftist organizations that ascribe different meanings to these concepts' and that '[b]uen vivir therefore represents a variety of discursive and practice-related "platforms"' (Kauffman & Martin, 2017, p. 130). The application of such inherently contestable terms is naturally problematic, and tools deployed to implement the concept of rights of nature in Ecuador are not only, or even mostly, legal; rather, they demonstrate the application of political tools to place pressure on the development of societal and legal norms.

The Ecuadorian Constitutional incorporation of rights of nature is in contradistinction to the conservative political complexion of recent administrations and public pressure arising from economic decline and growing crime. After Correa's exile to Belgium and sentence in absentia for corruption (Alexander, 2023), Guillermo Lasso, who favoured the privatisation of state assets and the expansion of mining and free trade, assumed office in May 2021 with an approval rating higher than

70% (Osborn, 2021). By August 2023, the nation was being described (by the previous President, Correa) as a 'failed state' after Lasso dissolved parliament (Forsans, 2023) and presidential candidate Fernando Villavicencio was assassinated. Lasso did not seek re-election and no candidate had a clear mandate after the first round of elections, prompting a second round that will occur in October between Luisa González and Daniel Noboa (Alexander, 2023). Both González, who is left-aligned, and Noboa, who is right-aligned, have canvassed on platforms of economic recovery. The election campaigns were held at the same time as referendums on mining in Chocó Andino and oil exploitation in Yasuní National Park. Despite the progressive assertion of the rights of nature, the political situation in Ecuador is not stable, and the constitutionally recognised rights of nature are neither fully implemented, easily interpreted nor guaranteed to survive another constitutional iteration.

Te Urewera and Te Awa Tupua (New Zealand)

Te Urewera is located on the North Island of Aotearoa/New Zealand between Hawke's Bay and the Bay of Plenty. It is a heavily forested, rugged and mountainous area characterised by beech forests. The area contains two large lakes, Waikaremoana and Waikereiti, and some smaller lakes, rivers and tributaries. The area has been continuously occupied by the Tūhoe peoples, although several other smaller groups also occupied the area. The Whanganui River (the context of Te Awa Tupua), also on the North Island, rises on Mount Tongariro, flowing to Taumarunui, King Country and Pirinki before reaching the coast at Whanganui. Te Urewera and the Whanganui River have been afforded the status of legal persons through legislation. Section 11(1) of the *Te Urewera Act 2014* (NZ) establishes Te Urewera as a legal person and the *Te Awa Tupua (Whanganui River Claims Settlement) Act 2017* (NZ) confers legal personhood on the Whanganui River.

The immediate context of legal recognition of Te Urewera and Te Awa Tupua in Aotearoa/New Zealand is a single-state democratic Western legal system formed after the colonisation of New Zealand from the mid-1800s. The Indigenous Māori were said to engage in 'shifting or so-called slash-and-burn' agriculture (Vayda, 1956) in an originally densely forested landscape and were also reported to engage in conquest between tribes for productive land. The Māori were recognised by the British government as occupying the land under the then common law presumption applying to inhabited lands. In those cases, there was 'no *ipso facto* abrogation of local laws and property rights' (McHugh, 1984). Māori laws would regulate Māori internal dealings, but English laws would apply to English people and to transactions and interactions between Māori and English (McHugh, 1984, p.236). The *Native Rights*

Act 1865 (NZ), supplemented by the *New Zealand Constitution Act 1852* s 71, were expressed to maintain Māori customary laws. McHugh argues that that s 71 amounts to an 'Imperial codification of the first aboriginal right at common law' (McHugh, 1984, p. 237, note 9).

Māori concepts of agricultural productivity and land conquest were no doubt acknowledged by colonisers, but that does not mean that there was a full understanding between the colonising forces (Pakeha) and the Māori. It could confidently be speculated that surface understandings may have disguised some of the deeper misunderstandings and mistranslations. After some initial uncertainties, the Treaty of Waitangi was signed by representatives of the British Crown and Māori leaders on behalf of their tribes. There are two versions of the treaty, and neither of which is a translation of the other (Stokes, 1992, p. 177). Perhaps unsurprisingly, since some concepts did not have a direct translation into the other language, this gave rise to fundamental misunderstandings and it has been noted that the concept of property, and its full set of 'incidents' under Māori tradition, may not have been fully translatable as legal incidents under English law.

As Banner notes, the British government recognised Māori property ownership and much of Aotearoa was acquired by purchase during the 19th century: '[in] 1800, the Māori had owned over 60 million acres of land; by 1911, they owned only 7 million, much of which was not well suited for farming' (Banner, 2000, p. 47). Banner notes that there were misunderstandings of the nature of land transactions at an individual level so that on many occasions there would have been bad bargains; there would also have been exertions of influence, harassment, duress or force of various degrees, but overall, Banner attributes the respective positions of the purchasers as functions of the market, in which the law was/is a servant. This was characteristic of the perceived role of law at the time: '[law] does not intervene in markets; law constitutes markets' (Banner, 2000, p. 50). The law of property and the law of contracts (including agency) are the fundamental building blocks of the market, and transactional law maintains the certainty of these legal constructs, but speculation in property values, particularly anticipating an influx of Pakeha agriculturalists, overwhelmingly benefited the purchasers of land to the comparative disadvantage of the vendor tribes.

The *Treaty of Waitangi Act 1975* (NZ) incorporated an English language and a Māori language version of the Treaty and created the Waitangi Tribunal to resolve outstanding Māori claims (see, e.g. Stokes, 1992). Overlying the issues of cession, of right to govern and of the reciprocal obligations as understood in the conventional English legal meaning of the text are issues of translation of the text of the Treaty. Although how the treaty was implemented during the colonial settlement of Aotearoa is considered to have prioritised the governance techniques of the colonisers, Māori aspirations for power-sharing have more recently advanced. Shared governance, co-governance, co-planning and co-management have been a feature of legislative frameworks for resource management for some time (Harmsworth et al., 2016), the core principles of which have been developed from statements of the Waitangi Tribunal. In this way, conceptualisations of land, water and the interaction between ecosystems and people not prioritised (or acknowledged) by contemporary Western property law can be articulated. Harmsworth et al. (2016) note that 'Te Ao Māori (Māori world view) and mātauranga Māori (Māori knowledge systems) refer to a wide range of cultural concepts, values, knowledge systems, frameworks, ethics, and principles'. Thus, for instance, management plans made pursuant to the *Resource Management Act 1991* (NZ) are required to state Māori values and thus enable collaboration and act as sites of knowledge.

Te Urewera includes the ancestral lands of the Tūhoe Māori. After colonisation, the area was established as a statutory reserve, with features of 'virtual Tūhoe home rule' (Webster, 2019, p. 191). However, Webster argues that 'by 1908 the relatively benevolent colonial policy that had established the [Urewera District Native Reserve] under Tūhoe control began to be reversed, and by 1915 it had become systematically subversive of the 1896 Act' (Webster, 2019, p. 194). The area was established as a National Park in 1954. It was administered through the usual succession of public authorities – in this case, the Department of Lands until 1986 and then the Department of Conservation. During this period, the area was 'protected' and harvesting of certain species (such as the kererū, a species of pigeon) was prohibited. This had a particular impact on the Ngāi Tūhoe for whom the bird is a taonga, or treasure, and 'from which the iwi draws part of its cultural identity' (Lyver et al., 2008, p. 7). In 2014, the National Park was disestablished by the *Te Urewera Act 2014* (NZ) as a result of the Ngāi Tūhoe Treaty of Waitangi settlement. Section 11(1) of the *Te Urewera Act 2014* (NZ) establishes Te Urewera as a legal entity with 'all the rights, powers, duties, and liabilities of a legal person'. Those rights, powers and duties are exercised by the Te Urewera Board in the manner required by the Act.

Under s 12 of the *Te Awa Tupua (Whanganui River Claims Settlement) Act 2017* (NZ) 'Te Awa Tupua is an indivisible and living whole, comprising the Whanganui River from the mountains to the sea, incorporating all its physical and metaphysical elements', and at s 14, the Act states that 'Te Awa Tupua is a legal person and has all the rights, powers, duties, and liabilities of a legal person'. In practical terms, s 11 of the legislation states that 'Te Pā Auroa is a relevant consideration in the exercise of all statutory functions, powers, and duties in relation to the Whanganui River or to activities in its catchment that affect the Whanganui River'. Statutory functions, powers and duties are required to be exercised consistently with the purpose of the legislation. Section 15 sets out the legal effect of the attribution of personhood: decision-makers must recognise, provide for and have particular regard to the Te Awa Tupua status; and utilise Kawa. Under s 17, Te Awa Tupua is also required to be given various particular forms of status under domestic legislation, so that it is, for instance, a public authority for the purposes of several pieces of legislation. It is capable of applying for registration as a charitable entity under legislation, a body corporate under s 188 of the *Resource Management Act 1991* and under s 17(d) is a 'registered collector of taonga tūturu for the purposes of section 14 of the *Protected Objects Act 1975*'. As in the case of other non-human persons, Te Awa Tupua has a 'human face' in Te Pou Tupua, established by s 18. Te Pou Tupua is to 'act and speak for and on behalf of Te Awa Tupua', along with other general and specific functions set out in s 19. An advisory group, Te Karewao, has been established to provide advice and support for Te Pou Tupua. The provisions of the Act in establishing personhood do not appear to create the equivalent of human rights in the river and ecosystem. Section 16 of the Act states that, unless otherwise expressly provided in the Act or in other legislation, the Act does not limit private property rights in the river or affect rights or interests in water, wild-life, fish, aquatic life, seaweeds or plants. At the current state of both international and domestic law, there is a fundamental incompatibility between the rights acknowledged in the human and the capacity to hold that human as property.

The *Te Urewera Act 2014* (NZ) utilises the Western construct of legal personality in relation to the river and surrounding ecosystems. As we have seen, the legislation creates a species of legal person not unlike a statutory corporation. The creation of rights and liabilities under the legislation does not necessarily track Māori cultural worldviews; rather it responsibilises the river and its environs with its own protection. The potential for the river to be sued is inherent in the provision of legal personality: as s 14 notes, Te Awa Tupua has the duties and liabilities of a legal person, as well as the rights. In some contexts, this will address issues of standing – that is, the capacity to bring legal proceedings to protect an interest. However, standing rules are various and the capacity to bring proceedings is entirely based on the nature of the proceedings. The idea of property conceptualised in the legislation is the English com-mon law idea:

> At its heart ... property remains an organising principle of Te Awa Tupua legislation. The fee simple estate in the Crown-owned parts of the bed of the Whanganui River vests in Te Awa Tupua [itself]. This land is inalienable, but an easement, lease, or licence may be granted on behalf of Te Awa Tupua for a term of less than 35 years. While

ownership of some minerals in the bed remains with the Crown, others vest in Te Awa Tupua. The Act also preserves a range of existing rights: public use and access rights and existing private property rights, including customary rights and title.

(Sanders, 2018, p. 231)

Ganges and Mother Earth (India)

Whereas in other jurisdictions, the avenue for the creation of juristic personhood has been through constitutional documents (including treaties), the significant aspect of the Indian approach is that it has occurred through case law (although in a particular constitutional context). The Ganges and Yamuna Rivers and Tributaries were granted legal personhood in *Mohd Salim v. State of Uttarakhand* (2017), as were lakes, glaciers, air, jungles, wetlands and other ecological sites in *Lalit Miglani v. State of Uttarakhand* (2017) (although the Supreme Court of India issued a stay of the High Court's order pending appeal). Personhood in nature draws upon cultural understandings not necessarily reduced to writing, as in the case of written constitutions and legislation. Accordingly, the Indian instance diverges from the rights jurisprudence arising in other cultures in arising primarily in case law.

Prior to colonisation, Indian kingdoms were legally pluralist (recognising the legal systems of more than one culture) and culturally deeply enmeshed – indeed, they have been described as 'subservient to society' (Maine, 1861). The colonisation of India by the British resulted in its transformation at a fundamental level:

Indian legal orders gradually changed from a plural system with a protected place for indigenous legal authorities to one dominated by a type of state law that relied heavily and increasingly on English legal texts, sources, and procedures [representing] nearly complete displacement of an indigenous legal system by a European legal order.

(Singh & Kumar, 2019, p. 1)

Whilst the Indian legal system bears a heavy colonial imprint, cultural, including religious, markers were not removed. Historically, the Hindu concept of 'dharma' invokes both legal and religious duties (Singh & Kumar, 2019, p. 2). Ancient pluralist law was supported by the Vedas (divine texts), Smritis (interpretations) and Achara (customs and practices), which bound even the monarch (Singh & Kumar, 2019, p. 2). The later influence of the Muslim Sultanate, incorporating certain Islamic laws, also recognised legal pluralism at the local level. The storied history of Indian law raises the question of whether it amounted to a theocracy, but a movement to separate state and religion preceded the

Western enlightenment movement by millennia (Singh & Kumar, 2019, p. 8), although it was not entirely successful given the role of Islamic law in some areas. For the purposes of this discussion, it is sufficient to note that at the time of British colonisation, Indian law already drew upon several cultural worldviews, tolerated a great deal of variation, particularly at local level, incorporated both formal and informal systems and regulated a highly diverse set of peoples. Singh and Kumar note that

> the legal 'chaos' and 'vacuum' often cited by Britishers in the early colonial era … was in actuality a highly evolved and complex legal system, perhaps so deeply connected with the socio-cultural needs and aspirations of the Indian populace that it could be easily mistaken to be a set of mere social norms enforced by an informal traditional court.
>
> (Singh & Kumar, 2019, p. 9)

The imposition of an alien single system on this complex juristic-cultural complex did result in a form of judicial administration (a common law hierarchy) that continues to exist. Of course, this is a massive simplification; the East India Company and its employees originally presided in some courts, and the arrangements in Calcutta were not the same as in other parts of the country. The unique position of the East India Company meant that courts were created to control the Company itself (Singh & Kumar, 2019, p. 12). The texture of governance also varied over time, with periods of 'liberal' administrators replaced by a 'strong hand' after the 1857 Indian Rebellion, and legal mechanisms and systems created specifically to deal with the problems caused by white settlement itself.

India has a written constitution, drafted by an elected Constituent Assembly, ratified in 1949 and effective from 26 January 1950, replacing the English *Government of India Act 1935* (UK). It has been described as 'the framework through which the world's largest and one of its most contentious democracies was brought into being … the charter through which an ancient civilisation was set on the road to modernity and radical social reform' (Choudhry et al., 2016, p. 1). Like most constitutional compacts, it is the result of a political project, but as Choudhry et al. note, this was not canvassed in the context of full social unanimity in norms and values. The constitution formed part of the process of forming agreement on certain social mores, but was also formed in the knowledge that disagreements, even fundamental ones, would continue; so, the constitutional framework would have to be robust enough to maintain institutions.

The immediate context of the formation of the constitutional framework was the process of becoming independent from British rule, so it was nationalist in that sense. However, it drew upon several influences, so formed 'an amalgam of many sources and traditions' (Choudhry et al., 2016, p. 5). It is based on a separation of powers and accordingly is concerned with 'the limits and constraints on public power, the ways in which the sovereignty of the people can be preserved against various usurpations' (Choudhry et al., 2016, p. 5). Having been settled in the post-war 'rights' era, it also recognises and protects human rights in the sense promulgated in international instruments (unlike, say, the constitutions of Australia and the United States).

The Indian Constitution is long and detailed and sets out obligations for both the State and individuals. Thus, in part 3 of the Constitution 'fundamental rights' are outlined, including the rights to life and personal liberty, equality, freedom of speech, education, rights against exploitation, freedom of religion and protection of minorities. The 'right to life' expressed in Article 21 has been judicially expanded to include a range of ancillary rights such as the right to water (Wahi, 2022), to health and the right to earn a livelihood. Article 48A deals with 'protection and improvement of environment and safeguarding of forests and wild life' and article 51A sets out 'fundamental duties' imposed on citizens '(g) to protect and improve the natural environment including forests, lakes, rivers and wild life, and to have compassion for living creatures'. District and metropolitan planning committees are obliged, in preparing draft development plans, to have regard to matters of common interest between the districts/municipalities and the Panchayats, including coordinated spatial planning, sharing of natural resources, the integrated development of infrastructure and conservation of the environment. Conversely, the regulation and development of interstate rivers are dealt with in Schedule 7, which deals with the division of powers between the Union and State governments. Development of interstate rivers is in the purview of the Union to the extent that it is 'declared by Parliament by law to be expedient in the public interest'.

International attention was focused on the move towards environmental personhood in India through the Ganga pollution cases. The Ganga (Padma in Bangladesh) originates in the Himalayas in Uttarakhand in Northern India and flows for over 2,500 kilometres, being joined by the Yamuna, Brahmaputra and Meghna rivers before its outflow in the Bay of Bengal. It passes through Uttarakhand, Uttar Pradesh, Bihar, Jharkhand and West Bengal, servicing over 400 million people (Dwivedi et al., 2018), including densely populated centres and industrial sites. Population is projected to increase in the Ganges River basin (Sharma et al., 2023, p. 17), increasing sources of pollution as well as demand, as the river is also used for irrigation and receives runoff from farmlands. The river has religious significance for the Hindu people, who worship the goddess Ganga and practices such as 'bathings and disposal of the remains of the dead' (Pathak & Mishra, 2020) occur in the river, highlighting its polluted state. Sharma et al. (2023, p. 2) note:

> Despite being the most sacred river in the Hindu culture, the Ganges is amongst the most polluted rivers in India as well as the world, mainly due to municipal and industrial wastes causing organic, inorganic and pathogenic pollution in the Ganges.

The severity of the pollution in the river resulted in the implementation of various projects by the Indian government; the 'Ganga River Basin Management Plan, National Commission on Integrated Water Resource Development Plan, River Development and Ganga Rejuvenation, and National Mission for Clean Ganga' (Sharma et al., 2023, p. 2). The Ganga Action Plan (GAP) intended to make the river 'fit for bathing' was formulated in 1985 (Tare et al., 2003) to address human pollutants arising from untreated domestic and industrial discharges into the river, including by the construction of wastewater treatment facilities. These various strategies have improved water quality and reduced levels of heavy metal contamination, but other pollutants remain, both geogenic and anthropogenic. Naturally occurring pollutants can also interact with anthropogenic-source pollutants or processes to exacerbate water quality problems.

The GAP coincided with the Ganga pollution cases (which commenced with *Mehta v. Union of India* (1988)). Chaturvedi (2019) notes that analysis of data from 1986–2004 identified a 'significant drop in river pollution' (Chaturvedi, 2019, p. 725). Whether that can be attributed to the case or the GAP is another matter; but in any event, the positive outcome prompted further cases. In *Jaiswal v. State of Uttar Pradesh* (1997), the court directed the government to regulate the dumping of corpses in the river, defecation on the banks of the river and the dumping of industrial waste with the creation of a 'river police force'. Several later cases built on the jurisprudence. In *Mohd Salim v. State of Uttarakhand* (2017), the Ganges and Yamuna Rivers and Tributaries were granted legal personhood, and in *Lalit Miglani v. State of Uttarakhand* (2017), other ecological sites such as lakes, glaciers, air, jungles and wetlands were ruled to have legal personhood. These cases have both been appealed and there is a stay on their implementation. Jolly and Memon (2021) note that the Uttarakhand State Government has cited a range of hurdles to implementation, including the cross-border effect of attempts at implementation and consequent potential liability.

Manoomin (United States)

Manoomin ('good seed'), or wild rice, was declared to have inherent rights pursuant to Treaty authority by the White Earth Band of Ojibwe in Minnesota (White Earth Band of Ojibwe, 2019). The Anishinaabeg are a cultural and language group residing on both the Canadian and American sides of the national border. The Ojibwe, Chippewa, Odawa, Algonquin, Nipissing, Mississauga, Oji-Cree and Metis are associated with the grouping. The White Earth Reservation in Minnesota is part of their treaty rights of the people and it is the United States' legal arrangements at issue here. The inherent rights of manoomin include the rights to exist, flourish, regenerate and evolve and its rights to restoration, recovery and preservation (White Earth Committee, 2018). This has been characterised as an attempt to protect it from 'industrial activities that harm water quality and introduce genetically modified organisms into the ecosystem' (Gellers, 2021). This development originated in a Tribal Resolution based on a Treaty between the White Earth Band and the colonising government. The law is also situated in a complex of Constitutional provisions, tribal negotiations and settlements, property and water law, including the detailed United States Constitutional cases on eminent domain and the United Nations Declaration on the Rights of Indigenous Peoples. The resolution contains a regulation, which makes it enforceable under tribal law (Gross, 2021) and it has also been cited in litigation related to the expansion of permitted water rights, pipeline construction and access seeking an injunction and declaration against the Minnesota Department of Natural Resources and the construction of an oil pipeline, although a lack of precedent resulted in dismissal of the tribe's claims.

The significance of manoomin is clear not only from cultural referents but also in law. Manoomin is referred to in Treaty documents (although not the 1867 Treaty). It is a grain that grows in water, usually slow-moving flows on the shores of lakes or the banks of streams, and is a staple of many of the tribes. It also features in ceremonial activities and sacred stories (Gross, 2021). The territories in which the tribes claimed rights for the manoomin included territories ceded under the 1867 treaty between the United States government and the Mississippi Band of Chippewa Indians (Kappler, 1929, pp. 974–976, cited in Gross, 2021, p. 132). The Treaty was not the only one between the United States and these groups as white settlement pushed tribes into less attractive lands to the north and they ceded large areas (Danziger, 1973, p. 176), but the 1867 Treaty had provided for the removal of the people to the reservation at White Earth (Treuer, 2011, p. 3) in exchange for ceded territories. The White Earth Reservation was comprised of 800,000 acres, which included

> prime farmland in the Red River Valley, valuable stands of pine timber, and lakes and streams supporting seasonal resources on which the Anishinaabeg had relied for generations [and] seemed

well suited to meet both subsistence needs and an evolving market orientation.

(Meyer, 1991, p. 368)

The period favoured assimilation strategies, including the marketisation of Reservation resources through the creation of private property rights and the *General Allotment Act 1887*, which enabled subdivision and settlement (Meyer, 1991, p. 368). However, Meyer argues that the relative market sophistication of the Anishinaabeg had encouraged the administration to permit landholding on a more liberal basis, enabling greater 'assimilation' of the tribes to the market economy, primarily through agriculture. The prevailing sentiment for both tribal and non-tribal settlement and occupation of the American inland was the desire to create self-sufficient 'yeoman' farmers – the Jeffersonian ideal, facilitated by the *Nelson Act 1889* that enabled land allotment. Meyer reports that during negotiations prior to the introduction of this Act, 'the US Chippewa Commission coerced a "cession" of four heavily forested townships from resident Indians' (Meyer, 1991, p. 381), enabling the operation of logging companies in the area. Subsequent construction of dams and use of waterways for transport in the logging process had a detrimental effect on traditional subsistence forms of agriculture by altering water flows, and this had a significant impact on the harvest of manoomin, washing out wild rice crops, inundating gardens, causing erosion, muddying streams and creating conditions for fire. 'What lumber companies regarded as nothing more than a necessary right-of-way took a decided toll on the subsistence economy' (Meyer, 1991, p. 382).

Policy favouring participation in the market also worked against subsistence and wider tribal interests. In common with allotment policies in other parts of the world, the land parcels were often too small for successful agriculture. Forest areas, at the time more valuable than other resources, were brought into the market as the *Indian Appropriations Act 1904* authorised the sale of timber. Meyer notes: '[t]hat Indian people should learn capitalistic acquisitiveness was deemed more important than equity and accurate implementation of established laws' (Meyer, 1991, p. 384), and those who had embraced these values were further supported by policy and legislation in the form of the *Burke Act 1906*, which enabled a move away from land in trust and a transition to freely alienable land and resources (although requiring representations regarding 'competency') (Meyer, 1991, p. 384). That there had been intermarriage between tribal members and other settlers was also considered a rationale for lifting restrictions through the 'Clapp Rider' to the legislation. This contentious addendum sought to bypass time-consuming competency hearings by removing restrictions on alienation from land held by 'adult mixed bloods' (Meyer, 1991, p. 384). This resulted in a period of rapid dealing in land parcels, claims of underhand methods by purchasers and brokers, and judicial and political contestation as to the meaning of 'mixed blood' in this context. Conversely, revenue from the sale of produce was kept in trust to fund social infrastructure on the reservation (schools, health services and so on) – Meyer (1991, p. 388) notes that by this mechanism tribal members effectively 'financed their own "assimilation"'. A complex pattern of demographic shift resulted in tribal members moving into settlements (away from means of subsistence), overcrowding and sharing accommodation. Non-tribal purchasers of land fenced and enclosed land and water sources, and interfered with seasonal food gathering. Food shortages and illness resulted. Meyer notes that by 1915 only 300 tribal members remained farming. Many members left White Earth.

Using the *Rights of Nature* as a model, the White Earth Band 'worked with the Community Environmental Legal Defense Fund (CELDF), with its International Center for the Rights of Nature, in the development of the draft law' (White Earth Band of Ojibwe, 2019). Under Resolution 2018-05 Manoomin is stated to have

> [i]nherent rights to exist, flourish, regenerate, and evolve, as well as inherent rights to restoration, recovery, and preservation. These rights include, but are not limited to, the right to pure water and freshwater habitat; the right to a healthy climate system and a natural environment free from human-caused global warming impacts and emissions; the right to be free from patenting; as well as rights to be free from infection, infestation, or drift by any means from genetically engineered organisms, trans-genetic risk seed, or other seeds that have been developed using methods other than traditional plant breeding.

Conversely, tribal members have the right to harvest, protect and save the seeds and these are described as 'usufructuary rights to gather food and earn a modest living' (White Earth Band of Ojibwe, 2019).

Wilip-gin Birrarung murron (Australia)

The legislation from Victoria, Australia, creates a governance structure for the management of the Yarra River as a 'living entity'. There has since been academic discussion to create a new legal concept to enable the recognition of rivers as 'ancestral persons' (Pelizzon et al., 2021). The *Yarra River Protection (Wilip-gin Birrarung murron) Act 2017* (Vic) ('*Yarra River Act*') applies to a river and its environs in the state of Victoria, Australia. Unlike some of the more ambitious statements of environmental personhood, the legislation framed for the greater protection of the Yarra River (*Birrarung*) does not ascribe legal personhood to the river. It does, however, recognise it as a 'living entity' and creates a statutory mechanism for its acknowledgement as such. The reason for the inclusion of this case study is that it illustrates the liminal aspect of the concept of personhood in non-humans and ascribes notions of 'rights' a 'voice' of the river, along with the cultural claims of Indigenous peoples (Wardle, 2021), but recognises the reality of managing competing uses of a highly developed urban river with multiple stakeholders. It has been described as 'a new scheme and model for governance' of waterways using strategic planning concepts with input from traditional owner groups.

The Yarra River rises at Mount Baw Baw to flow 250 kilometres from the Great Dividing Range, through the Yarra Ranges to Port Phillip Bay. The river is a major feature of Melbourne, the capital city of Victoria, and remains the major source of the city's water. Recent urban renewal projects have capitalised on the site and amenity of the river; the Southbank development converted a previously industrial area to a densely populated living and office suburb. Melbourne Docklands, previously swampland and then an industrial dock facility, has similarly been converted into an inner-city suburb in a project conceptualised in the 1990s and still in development. These are high-profile and strategic projects with notable political importance. This is a significant reality in the context of the competing priorities of the river and its people.

Norris (2021) notes that two indigenous groups were occupying the area that is now Melbourne: the Boon wurrung and the Woi wurrung. In these groups were several clans and the Yarra River was called *Birrarung* in their language. An account of the indigenous understanding of the river and its environs was set out by Wurundjeri Council (which was a predecessor of the Wurundjeri Woi wurrung Cultural Heritage Corporation) in the forward to the Victorian Government's 2017 Yarra River Action Plan:

> Our Dreaming tells us that Bunjil, our Creator spirit made kulin (men) from the earth and that Bunjil's brother, Balliyang, the Bat, created bagarook (women) from the water. The requirement to touch the land and waterways lightly, respecting that which provides life, is implicit here. Since our beginning it has been understood that a harm to any aspect of biik, to Country, is a harm to all things and ourselves.

The Yarra River governance framework is based partially on the role of Indigenous people in the custodianship of the river and its environment, and this is set out in s 12 of the Act, which requires that 'Aboriginal cultural values, heritage and knowledge of Yarra River land should be acknowledged, reflected, protected and promoted' (s 12(2)) and that the role of traditional owners acknowledged 'through partnership, representation and involvement in policy planning and decision-making' (s 12(2)). Alongside this, however, s 12(3) requires that the 'cultural diversity and heritage of post-European settlement communities should be recognised and protected as a valued contribution to the identity, amenity and use of Yarra River land'. The Act requires, therefore, that the heritage of the settled community is to be considered alongside the interests of the river and its environs, and the experience and knowledge of a pre-settler river.

British colonisation of the Australian continent commenced around 1788 with the establishment of a penal colony in what is now New South Wales. The basis upon which colonisation occurred (and a feature legally distinguishing the Australian colonies from New Zealand, and indeed other British colonies during that period; Banner, 2005) was the principle of *terra nullius* – a designation that the land was empty, or unowned. In *Attorney General v. Brown* (1847), the New South Wales Full Court (as it then was) held that wastelands in the Colony 'are and ever have been, from the time of its first settlement in 1788, in the Crown' (*Attorney General v. Brown*, 1847, p. 316) (thus applying the feudal principles arising in English property law to the colony). In *Cooper v. Stuart* (1889), Lord Watson in the Privy Council asserted that in 1788 Australia fell within the class of a Colony acquired by peaceful annexation, being 'a tract of territory practically unoccupied, without settled inhabitants or settled law' (*Cooper v. Stuart*, 1889, para. [11]). Windeyer described the position as it was understood in 1957:

> The title of the British Crown to the continent of Australia in public international law arose by acquisition as a territory not formerly part of the dominions of any civilized state. It was made a part of the British Empire by occupation, not by conquest or cession.
>
> (Windeyer, 1957)

Although the designation of *terra nullius* was judicially refuted in *Mabo v. Queensland (No 2)* (1992), its implications had real legal significance to the acknowledgement of the law of Indigenous people and to the reception of English law in Australia, and more prosaically to the radical title of the Crown in Australia from which other title to land (other than native title) was derived.

That the land was considered *terra nullius* for the purposes of the reception of English law, even though New Zealand, settled after Australia, was not, appears to be partly a result of the contemporary observations of the very small number of Indigenous people observed, along with the capacity of the land to sustain a population of any significance. In *Coe v. Commonwealth* (1979), Murphy J notes that 'the most consistently mentioned number of aboriginal people' at the time of settlement was estimated to be 300,000. Banner (2005) suggests that this is consistent with de Vattel's (1760) view that there was no necessity to purchase the land from the original inhabitants because such a small number could not have ownership of such a vast area. It is now legally established that the assertion of *terra nullius* was based on incorrect information. The application of *terra nullius* was explicitly considered by the Australian High Court in *Mabo v. Queensland (No 2)* (1992) in which the Court traced the origin of the fiction of *terra nullius* in its application to Australia. The outcome of *Mabo* was the recognition of native title to land where it had not been extinguished, although that title did not amount to a property right as it is understood in English law. Later cases, *Western Australia v. Ward* (2002) and *Members of the Yorta Yorta Aboriginal Community v. Victoria* (2002), further expanded on the extent of native title. The effect of *Mabo* on heavily settled lands such as Melbourne was limited, and in any event, legislation was quickly passed to modify the effect of the case. The *Native Title Act* 1993 (Cth) created a procedural infrastructure to assess claims to native title and provided a set of specified native title rights in the event of a successful claim, and currently around 54% of Australian land is held by Aboriginal and Torres Strait Islander communities under either exclusive or non-exclusive title (Nicholas et al., 2021) – non-exclusive titles include pastoral leases, which are a common form of interest in large scale agricultural operations in the Australian outback.

The area around the Yarra River has been extensively changed since European settlement. Melbourne was settled by Europeans in 1835, but settlement was accelerated by the discovery of gold in 1851. Infrastructure for water supply, sewerage and drainage commenced in 1857 to serve the growing population (Ferguson et al., 2013, p. 7303). The Yan Yean Reservoir was constructed in 1857, followed by the Upper Yarra Dam in 1957 (Leahy et al., 2005, p. 132). The Thomson Reservoir, which followed the drought of 1982–1983, was meant to 'drought proof' the city (Ferguson et al., 2013, p. 7303), which had continued to grow – it had a population of 2.9 million in 1982 and 5.2 million in 2023. Greater Melbourne is projected to reach a population of 9 million in 2056 (Phelps et al., 2023, p. 134). Along with water infrastructure, settlement imperatives resulted in land reclamation – in its natural state, parts of the river descended into swamp, and in other parts, the river spread over the floodplain, which was infilled during settlement (Mitchell et al., 1996). Erosion increased river turbidity (Leahy et al., 2005, p. 131) and the floodplains contracted. Regulation of the river with the construction of dams reduced the number of flooding events. At present, the upper catchment is preserved and is regarded as 'relatively pristine' but the middle and lower parts of the Yarra range in quality from good to poor (Leahy et al., 2005, p. 131).

The purposes of the *Yarra River Act* are, *inter alia*, to 'provide for the declaration of the Yarra River and certain public land in its vicinity for the purpose of protecting it as one living and integrated natural entity' (s 1(a)), to establish an advisory body to the Minister (the Birrarung Council) in relation to the use and development of Yarra River land (s 1(c)) and to create the Greater Yarra Urban Parklands as a 'state significant urban natural entity' (s 1(c)). Other purposes relate to processes such as the development of the Yarra Strategic Plan (s 1(c)). The objects of the Act, listed in s 5, include recognition of the importance of the River and its environs 'to the economic prosperity, vitality and liveability of Melbourne and the Yarra Valley', referring particularly to ecological health, but also 'the cultural, social, environmental and amenity values of the Yarra River and the landscape in which the Yarra River is situated' (s 5(a)(i))) and 'the environmental significance of the biodiversity corridor along the Yarra River (s 5(a)(ii)). In other words, whilst the Act declares parts of the river and certain parts of the surrounding environment as 'one living and integrated natural entity' and has as its objects the protection of that entity, it does not constitute the entirety of the environment of the Yarra River, nor explicitly create legal personhood in the River. Moreover, it explicitly cites the priorities of the entity within a spectrum of other anthropogenic priorities; not merely the survival requirements of the population, but also growth needs such as esteem and self-actualisation served by cultural, social and amenity values of the river. The 'Yarra Protection Principles' are set out in part 2 of the Act, and are divided into 'general', 'environmental', 'social', 'recreational', 'cultural' and 'management' principles. Section 7 requires that *proposed* development and decision-making 'should' be 'based on the effective integration of environmental, social and cultural considerations in order to improve public health and wellbeing and environmental benefit'. The relative weighting of each of these considerations is not clear.

The *Yarra River Act* was enacted by a state in a federation with shared legislative capacities partially defined in a written federal constitution enacted by the UK in the *Commonwealth of Australia Constitution Act 1900* (UK). The state *Water Act 1989* (Vic), which sets up the governance framework for water management and use in Victoria, is the primary source of law relating to water governance and sets up a marketised framework consistent with both state and federal water policy (and public sector policy generally). Water entitlements are 'shares' of the available resource (which may amount to very little in a dry year), and environmental water can be held separately by organisations such as the Victorian Environmental Water Holder and the Commonwealth

Environmental Water Holder. O'Donnell notes that the '[e]nvironmental water in the Yarra catchment continues to be held by the Victorian Environmental Water Holder, an entity which is not formally required to be involved in or endorse the Yarra Strategic Plan' (O'Donnell, 2020, p. 653).

It is still too early to assess the impact of the legislation on the river except to say that it will be largely at the level of integrated land planning. The governance framework established by the Act carves out an exception to the statewide planning practices established by the *Planning and Environment Act 1987* (Vic), and since the water allocation framework is governed separately (and water entitlements are held by different persons), the *Yarra River Act* does not explicitly guarantee a flow of water (O'Donnell, 2020).

References

Alexander, I. (2023, August 25). Ecuador election: As run-off looms, voters crave genuine change. *Al Jazeera*. https://www.aljazeera.com/news/2023/8/25/ecuador-election-as-run-off-looms-voters-crave-genuine-change

Attorney General v. Brown (1847) 2 SCR (NSW) App 3.

Banner, S. (2000). Conquest by contract: Wealth transfer and land market structure in colonial New Zealand. *Law and Society Review*, *34*(1), 47.

Banner, S. (2005). Why terra nullius? Anthropology and property law in early Australia. *Law and History Review*, *23*(1), 95.

Becker, M. (2011). Correa, indigenous movements, and the writing of a new constitution in Ecuador. *Latin American Perspectives*, *38*(1), 47–62.

Berros, M. V. (2017). Defending rivers: Vilcabamba in the South of Ecuador. *RCC Perspectives*, *6*, 37–44.

Burke Act 1906 U.S. Statutes at Large, 33.

Chaturvedi, I. (2019). Why the Ganga should not claim a right of the river. *Water International*, *44*(6–7), 719–735. https://doi.org/10.1080/02508060.2019.1679947

Choudhry, S., Khosla, M., & Bhanu, P. B. (2016). *The Oxford handbook of the Indian constitution*. Oxford University Press.

Coe v. Commonwealth (1979) 24 ALR 118.

Commonwealth of Australia Constitution Act 1900 (UK).

Cooper v. Stuart (1889) 14 AC 286.

Danziger, E. J. Jr. (1973). They would not be moved: The Chippewa Treaty of 1854. *Minnesota Historical Society Press*, *43*(5), 175–185.

de Vattel, E. (1760). *Law of nations* (English translation).

Delgado, M. A. (2022). Reviewing climate change and the rights of nature: A Colombian example through an international perspective. *Revista Catalana de Dret Ambiental*, *13*(2), 1–44.

Dwivedi, S., Mishra, S., Seema, T., & Deo, R. (2018). Ganga water pollution: A potential health threat to inhabitants of Ganga basin. *Environment International*, *117*, 327–338. https://doi.org/10.1016/j.envint.2018.05.015.

Ferguson, B. C., Brown, R. R., Frantzeskaki, N., de Haan, F. J., & Deletic, A. (2013). The enabling institutional context for integrated water management: Lessons from Melbourne. *Water Research*, 47(20), 7300–7314. https://doi.org /10.1016/j.watres.2013.09.045

Forsans, N. (2023, August 16). Ecuador: How this 'island of peace' in Latin America has become a hotbed of violence run by criminal gangs and drug cartels. *The Conversation*. https://theconversation.com/ecuador-how-this -island-of-peace-in-latin-america-has-become-a-hotbed-of-violence-run-by -criminal-gangs-and-drug-cartels-211458

Gellers, J. C. (2021). *Rights for robots*. Routledge.

Government of India Act 1935 (UK).

Gross, L. W. (2021). The resolution by the white earth Anishinaabe nation to protect the inherent rights of wild rice. In J. C. Spee, A. McMurray, & M. McMillan (Eds.), *Clan and tribal perspectives on social, economic and environmental sustainability* (pp. 131–140). Emerald Publishing Limited.

Harmsworth, G., Awatere, S., & Robb, M. (2016). Indigenous Māori values and perspectives to inform freshwater management in Aotearoa-New Zealand. *Ecology and Society*, 21(4), 9.

Head, J. W. (1978). The challenge of international environmental management: A critique of the United Nations Environment Programme. *Virginia Journal of International Law*, 18(2), 269.

Jolly, S., & Menon, K. (2021). Of ebbs and flows: Understanding the legal consequences of granting personhood to natural entities in India. *Transnational Environmental Law*, 10(3), 467–492. https://doi.org/10.1017/ S2047102520000424

Kappler, C. J. (Ed.). (1929). *Indian affairs: Laws and treaties* (Vol. 2). Government Printing Office.

Kauffman, C. M., & Martin, P. L. (2017). Can rights of nature make development more sustainable? Why some Ecuadorian lawsuits succeed and others fail. *World Development*, 92, 130–142.

Lalit Miglani v. State of Uttarakhand (2017, March 30) Writ Petition (PIL) No.140 of 2015. High Court of Uttarakhand at Nainital.

Leahy, P. J., Tibby, J., John, K., Peter, A., Heijnis, H., & Kershaw, J. S. (2005). The impact of European settlement on Bolin Billabong, a Yarra River floodplain lake, Melbourne, Australia. *River Research and Applications*, 21(2–3), 131–149.

Lyver, P. O'B., Taputu, T. M., Kutia, S. T., & Brenda, T. (2008). Tūhoe Tuawhenua mātauranga of kererū (Hemiphaga novaseelandiae novaseelandiae) in Te Urewera. *New Zealand Journal of Ecology*, 32(1), 7–17.

Mabo v. Queensland (No 2) (1992) 175 CLR 1.

Maine, H. S. (1861). *Ancient law: Its connection with the early history of society, and its relation to modern ideas*. John Murray.

McBurney, M., Tuaza, L. A., & Johnson, C. (2022). Paying for ecological services in Ecuador: The political economy of structural inequality. *Journal of Agrarian Change*, 385–403.

McHugh, P. G. (1984). Aboriginal title in New Zealand courts. *Canterbury Law Review*, 2(2), 235.

Mehta v. Union of India and Others (1988) AIR 1115.

Members of the Yorta Yorta Aboriginal Community v. Victoria (2002) 194 ALR 538.

Meyer, M. L. (1991). "We can not get a living as we used to": Dispossession and the white earth Anishinaabeg, 1889–1920. *American Historical Review*, 96(2), 368–394.

Mitchell, P., Bennison, G., Eliezer, K., Hedger, M., Lloyd, L., McGuckin, J., Moore, S., Cook, D. & Craigie, N. (1996). *A study of three Yarra Billabongs in Yarra Valley Parklands*. Melbourne Parks and Waterways.

Mohd Salim v. State of Uttarakhand (2017, March 20). Writ Petition (PIL) No.126 of 2014. High Court of Uttarakhand at Nainital.

Native Rights Act 1865 (NZ).

Native Title Act 1993 (Cth).

Nelson Act 1889.

Nicholas, J., Wahlquist, C., Ball, A., & Evershed, N. (2021, May 17). Who owns Australia? *The Guardian*. https://www.theguardian.com/australia-news/ng -interactive/2021/may/17/who-owns-australia

Norris, J. (2021). The naming of the Yarra River as an act of colonialism. *Agora*, 56(3), 59.

O'Donnell, E. (2020). Rivers as living beings: Rights in law, but no rights to water? *Griffith Law Review*, 29(4), 643–668.

Osborn, C. (2021, August 27). A savvy start for Ecuador's new president. *Foreign Policy Magazine*. https://foreignpolicy.com/2021/08/27/ecuadors-president -guillermo-lasso-pandemic-indigenous-rights/

Pathak, S. S., & Mishra, P. (2020). A review of the Ganga River water pollution along major urban centres in the state of Uttar Pradesh, India. *International Research Journal of Engineering and Technology*, 7(3), 1202–1210.

Pelizzon, A., O'Donnell, Dr E., & Poelina, Dr A. (2021, October 18). Australia's rivers are ancestral beings. *Pursuit*. https://pursuit.unimelb.edu.au/articles/ australia-s-rivers-are-ancestral-beings

Phelps, N. A., Buxton, M., & Nichols, D. (2023). Melbourne's suburban landscapes: Administering population and employment growth. *Built Environment*, 49(1), 132–149. https://doi.org/10.2148/benv.49.1.132

Planning and Environment Act 1987 (Vic).

Protected Objects Act 1975 (NZ).

Resource Management Act 1991 (NZ).

RK Jaiswal v. State of Uttar Pradesh (1997) (Civil Misc. Writ Petition no. 21552 of 1997).

Sanders, K. (2018). Beyond human ownership? Property, power and legal personality for nature in Aotearoa New Zealand. *Journal of Environmental Law*, 30, 207.

Sharma, N., Liang, M.-C., Laskar, A. H., Huang, K.-F., Maurya, N. S., Singh, V., Ranjan, R., & Maurya, A. S. (2023). Basin-scale geochemical assessment of water quality in the Ganges River during the dry season. *Water*, 15(11), 2026. https://doi.org/10.3390/w15112026

Singh, M. P., & Kumar, N. (2019). *The Indian legal system: An enquiry* (Delhi, Online edn, Oxford Academic, April 17, 2019). Retrieved June 7, 2023, from https://doi.org/10.1093/oso/9780199489879.002.0004

Stokes, E. (1992). The Treaty of Waitangi and the Waitangi Tribunal: Māori claims in New Zealand. *Applied Geography, 12*(2), 176–191.

Tare, V., Bose, P., & Gupta, S. K. (2003). Suggestions for a modified approach towards implementation and assessment of Ganga Action Plan and other similar river action plans in India. *Water Quality Resources Journal of Canada, 38*(4), 607–626.

Te Awa Tupua (Whanganui River Claims Settlement) Act 2017 (NZ).

Te Urewera Act 2014 (NZ).

Treaty of Waitangi Act 1975 (NZ).

Treuer, A. (2011). *The assassination of Hole in the day.* Borealis Books.

Universal Declaration of the Rights of Mother Earth, 2010, Bolivia; *Framework Act on Mother Earth and Holistic Development to Live Well,* 2012, Bolivia.

Vayda, A. P. (1956). Maori conquests in relation to the New Zealand environment. *Journal of the Polynesian Society, 65*(3), 204–211

Wahi, N. (2022). The evolution of the right to water in India. *Water, 14*(3), 398. https://doi.org/ 10.3390/w14030398

Wardle, D. (2021). Sustainable indigenous water rights. In James C. Spee, Adela McMurray, and Mark McMillan (eds.), *Clan and tribal perspectives on social, economic and environmental sustainability,* (pp. 9–22). Emerald Insights.

Water Act 1989 (Vic).

Webster, S. (2019). Ōhāua te Rangi and reconciliation in Te Urewera, 1913–1983. *Journal of the Polynesian Society, 128*(2), 191–224.

Western Australia v. Ward (2002) 191 ALR 1.

Wheeler v. Director de la Procuraduria General del Estado en Loja (2011). *Corte provincial de justicia de Loja,* Judgment no. 11121-2011-0010.

White Earth Band of Ojibwe. (2019). *Chippewa establish rights of manoomin on white earth reservation and throughout 1855 ceded territory* (Media Statement). https://perma.cc/A3PUPBAL

White Earth Reservation Business Committee Resolution. (2018). Nos. 001-19-009 and 001-19-010; the 1855 treaty authority's resolution No. 2018-05.

Windeyer, W. J. V. (1957). *Lectures in legal history.* Law Book Co.

Yarra River Protection (Wilip-gin Birrarung murron) Act 2017 (Vic).

Chapter 4

Themes and contradictions

Introduction

Advocacy for environmental personhood draws upon many traditions and is scaffolded by narrative frameworks developed in those traditions. Many arguments claim resonance across quite disparate legal systems and cultural contexts, but as we have seen, formal legal legitimation techniques are needed when applied to a particular jurisdiction. The issues arising from the acceptance of some narrative frameworks raise contradictions central to the legitimacy of legal systems generally and remind us that environmental personhood owes part of its lineage to the critical legal studies movement as discussed in Chapter 1. The tension between the aims of critical legal studies and the coherence of law is, therefore, part of a wider discussion and is not able to be resolved here (and nor is ever likely to be resolved). Nevertheless, the popularity of tactics that undermine the premises on which law is based does justify a reminder: where traditional sources of legitimacy in law lose purchase, some alternative arguments for legitimacy will be required. It should be recalled that in many cases the application of law is an application of force against the individual, either in the form of action against the person's body or against their property or other ancillary rights. It has long been argued that if the law loses its perceived legitimacy, it risks widespread loss of authority and consequent civil unrest.

Legal pluralism

One of the themes arising from the ascription of legal personhood to the environment is the discursive framework surrounding legal pluralism. Legal pluralism is a natural concomitant to state legal systems incorporating indigenous ontologies and worldviews that may be inconsistent with the legal frameworks and systems of the colonising state. This is represented in a general shift to recognition of the right of indigenous

DOI: 10.4324/9781003388272-4

groups to autonomy, including 'rights to distinct nationalities, self-government, and self-determination' (Angstadt, 2016, p. 349). India's constitution was built upon not only colonisation but a pre-colonisation amalgam of social and cultural differences. Ecuador has been cited as an example of legal pluralism – originally the area now designated as the Republic of Ecuador was made up of several indigenous groups, which became part of the Incan Empire. Although colonised by Spain, the region achieved sovereignty in 1830. The current Constitution permits a degree of pluralism (Art 57 cl 10). New Zealand and US treaties recognised some aspects of legal pluralism within specified circumstances or geographical limits. Legal pluralism in Victoria, Australia, is limited, but remains a live issue – the Yoorrook Justice Commission report (2023) advocates several points at which legal treatment of Indigenous peoples should be differentiated from non-Indigenous peoples.

In acknowledging legal personhood in nature, a different form of pluralism arises that 'decentre[s] anthropocentric thinking on the environment and decentre[s] the state in the development of Earth-law' (Dancer, 2021, p. 23), however, the pluralism indicated by ecocentrism occurs alongside the legal pluralist arguments that justify many of the current environmental personhood claims. The Ecuadorian case study explicitly grounds the legitimacy of environmental personhood in indigenous ontologies, and other case studies also draw upon indigenous law and/or lore as at least supporting personhood claims.

References to indigenous ontologies arise particularly from the application of the colonialism lens to environmental scholarship, a matter to be considered below. They are also useful in providing a resistance narrative to support environmental advocacy. This is not a new argument; the consideration of the degree to which indigenous legal concepts and practices can be incorporated into a colonising law has been recorded since at least the time of the Roman empire. Thomas notes that local customs were typically given effect by the Romans

> but in an essentially ancillary capacity: eg, determining rates of interest, interpreting bonae fidei contracts and legacies and for local administrative matters. Respect for these last is surely no more than sound governmental principle – keep to local practice as far as possible.
> (Thomas, 1963, p. 44)

The local rules and practices were, in essence, maintained in specific areas where they were not inconsistent with the colonising law. Even so, the question of legitimacy arose, and the continued application of local customs was justified based on the 'tacit consent' of the local people (Thomas, 1963, p. 45), just as the Roman law was based on express consent. Whilst colonising law varied over time and place as to the level of acceptance of cultural mores into law (and keeping in mind that the distinction between law and culture, although acknowledged, can be difficult to draw in practice), the colonising law would typically override custom where the custom was in 'repugnant' to the settler law, or if it was expressly overruled. Advocacy for the adoption of customary laws which are repugnant in the legal sense can be problematic since it can give rise to issues of legitimacy within the rights framework being asserted. Even in 2023, an Australian court heard from a traditional elder that a person who had committed a crime would, in tribal law, 'be beaten or speared in the leg and then attend the victim's funeral' (Hams, 2023).

In some areas, it is possible to draw clear jurisdictional boundaries around areas in which cultural norms related to the environment are given force. In other areas, where custom has been overridden by explicit law or where the population is a mix of Indigenous and non-Indigenous people, as in the examples from Australia, New Zealand and the United States, more complex issues of legitimacy arise. Where traditional cultural concepts are intended to be inserted into an area with an imposed law, the process may have the effect of creating a jurisdictional cul-de-sac for several related reasons; first, the use of legal techniques to protect the environment is premised upon the exertion of power within a jurisdictional framework. Second, whereas pluralist legal forms are acknowledged in some legal systems, it is conceptually problematic, outside a bounded area, to use Western legal tools and concepts to protect elements of an alternative legal system and not others. The New Zealand and Victorian legislation creating environmental personhood or 'legal entity' status do not have the effect of reimposing indigenous cultural concepts, but rather integrate a pale form of indigenous cultural practice, superimposing parliamentary legitimacy over the previous religious or cultural forms of legitimacy. This avoids the problematic demands of legal pluralism. Additional logic issues arise from the common tendency (evident in the case studies) to identify as equivalent the ontologies of Indigenous peoples and ecosystem requirements, either now or in the future. Critiques of the approach suggest that the 'judicial hybrids' created by bringing various traditions together involve a 'mistranslation or cooptation of various traditions, values, and perspectives, particularly those of indigenous peoples' (Angstadt & Hourdequin, 2021, p. 29).

Aside from adopting legal pluralism to incorporate non-dominant worldviews, in the advocacy for legal personhood, we see the entanglement of two concepts – recognition of indigenous worldviews and an ecocentric approach to the environment. The advocacy for the incorporation of indigenous viewpoints appears at odds with an ecocentric attitude to the environment and its use. In some analyses, the tension is resolved by the argument that indigenous viewpoints recognise the interconnectedness of people and nature. Schimmöller (2020), for instance, states that 'Indigenous traditions, for centuries, have acknowledged the intrinsic value of nature as they recognize human beings as part of their interconnected surroundings' (Schimmöller, 2020, p. 570). Chaturvedi (2019, p. 723, citing Nash, 1989) argues that '[n]ative American religions and ethnic systems did not recognize a duality between man and nature'. Some recognise spirits or power inhabiting certain places (White, 2018, p. 131). Rose (1996, p. 7) argues that for the Australian Indigenous people/s, 'country' is

> not only a common noun but also a proper noun. People talk about country in the same way that they would talk about a person: they speak to country, sing to country, visit country, worry about country, feel sorry for country, and long for country. People say that country knows, hears, smells, takes notice, takes care, is sorry or happy. Country is not a generalised or undifferentiated type of place … Rather, country is a living entity with a yesterday, today and tomorrow, with a consciousness, and a will toward life.

Norman (2017), citing Cajete (2000) argues that the 'very cosmology of Indigenous Peoples is built on the intricate knowledge of and connection to their ancestral land – and all its relations, including its animals, plants, and water' (Norman, 2017, p. 537). She also extends this argument to ideas of jurisdictional authority: 'fixed (and policed) jurisdictions established through North American settler-colonial reservation and nation-state systems are in direct opposition to the intricate and reflexive relationships that Indigenous communities have with the natural world' (Norman, 2017, p. 537).

In a deeper sense, the utilisation of indigenous viewpoints to support environmental personhood appears to be a reaction to Enlightenment rationality. The separation of law from cultural mores arising from religion – secularism – is not a common subject for debate in Western states. The pre-Enlightenment entanglement of law and mythological worldviews should not be disentangled only for certain ontologies, and not others – or should it? Singh (2010) identifies strains of recent thought, from post-modernism, which tends to 'disdain the Enlightenment as biased, facile, self-deluded, over-optimistic, Eurocentric, imperialistic, and ultimately destructive' (Israel, 2006), to anti-modernists, who consider the Enlightenment as 'a tool to obscure non-European history while helping the legitimisation of colonisation' (Singh, 2010, p. 5).

There is an attraction to establishing (or attempting to establish) the moral claims of non-humans, particularly those aspects of the environment vulnerable to resource extraction. Establishing and elevating normative claims of non-humans is logical and, in essence, a sensible narrative extension even had the only issue been the existence of our own species. However, to do so may be to fall into two logic traps. First, to assert a moral basis for environmental claims is to re-elevate unsubstantiated meta-ethical claims, which should justify consideration of a range of other religious views that contain antithetical principles, including indigenous religious principles. Second, should the environment have moral arguments on its own behalf, what of incompatible value claims within the environment? For instance, where an indigenous environment is under threat from a non-indigenous but naturalised species, why is priority given to either species if both have equivalent moral claims? If their moral claims are not equivalent, who is to undertake the role of arbitration and remediation? It is well understood that environments are in a constant state of evolution as conditions change, even up to the point of mass extinction, without human input. As scientific knowledge improves, it may be possible to calculate the future of the environment absenting human impacts, and thus neutralise the human impact to watch a species diminish to eventual extinction – is that the moral outcome sought, even where a species has legal personhood? If that requires funding, what are the grounds for the legitimacy of taxation of humans to forward that goal? If the grounds for legitimacy are the preservation of our own species, then priority would be given to productive food crops rather than unproductive land uses – and so on. Legitimacy in modern state frameworks often appears tedious and bloodless; seeking to legitimise normative claims on the basis of a Pachamama who 'would cause earthquakes to remind the people to honor her' (White, 2018, p. 140) or to whose anger is attributed volcanic activity (White, 2018, p. 140) may introduce more elemental problems and problematic solutions.

A related conundrum is addressed by Ewering and Vetter (2023) who note that Germany has no indigenous population, unlike Ecuador, so the question arises whether it really needs rights of nature. Should heavily developed countries retrofit what is known of the indigenous worldviews applicable in each geographical region and apply it on the premise that this ontology will necessarily have environmentally better outcomes? Is that even jurisdictionally possible where political boundaries have been drawn and redrawn so many times? And which indigenous worldview is to be preferred? Where nature has been subject to the actions of a series of different worldviews over millennia, which group's worldview will be applied? Is it permissible to interrogate the ecological practices of extant groups of Indigenous peoples, or are they to be considered incontrovertible, both in relation to the existence or history of the practice and/or in relation to its environmental benefit? Chaturvedi (2019, p. 732) notes that, at least in the Indian context, the adherence to creation is not intended to be restorative of the environment but an expression of dharma, or duty. Indeed, she notes that 'the holiness of the Ganga has not been a successful deterrent to its continued obscene pollution' (Chaturvedi, 2019, p. 732); an insight given additional weight by the fact that, at least in some part, traditional practices add to river pollution. If indigenous viewpoints, once established, are incontrovertible, is this just replacing one form of anthropocentrism with another? In privileging ontologies in which science and religion are enmeshed in a legal culture are we returning to pre-Enlightenment worldviews in their entirety, or are we picking only certain aspects? And who has the right or capacity to make those choices, and on what authority?

A logic problem arising in private law (the law dealing with disputes between persons, including the law of contract and tort) is the implication arising from situating the personhood of nature outside the state through the incorporation of indigenous ontologies – perhaps a philosophical position but challenging in the context of utilising state infrastructure in support of claims of nature. The legislative incorporation of Māori belief systems and cultural practices in the manner set out in the *Te Urewera Act 2014* (NZ) and the *Te Awa Tupua (Whanganui River Claims Settlement) Act 2017* (NZ) continues a trajectory of recognition of Māori law consistent with the principles of settlement, enabled in particular as the land was unalienated. However, this understanding is embedded in and interacts with a legislative and judicial infrastructure which draws legitimacy from democratic mandate and almost inevitably defines the nature of the environment in terms capable of contemporary legal definition. The process of definition, which is unavoidable where individual rights are capable of contestation, forces the segregation, limitation and refinement of concepts. Similarly, the *Yarra River Act 2017* (Vic) creates a set of mechanisms for the management of the river environment that ally the management of the river with modern techniques of governance, although they also incorporate 'co-management' principles. To an extent, they replace already existing governance principles that incorporate indigenous viewpoints: the creation of a designated advisory body is not dissimilar to the long-established Catchment Management Authorities (CMAs), created under s 11 of the *Catchment and Land Protection Act 1994* (Vic). The objectives of that Act are to 'establish a framework for the integrated and co-ordinated management of catchments' (s 4(a)). Each of these CMAs are body corporates (persons in law) and are responsible for the preparation of regional catchment strategies for their regions (s 12). They are specifically required to include 'representatives of specified Aboriginal parties, in preparing and implementing the strategy and special area plans and in furthering the objectives of this Act' (s 12(c)). They have a central position as 'referral authorities' in Victorian planning law (under the *Planning and Environment Act 1987* (Vic)). Indeed, they can appeal against decisions of local authorities to grant permits under s 82 of the Act (see, for instance, *West Gippsland Catchment Management Authority v. South Gippsland SC* (2017) and *West Gippsland Catchment Management Authority v. East Gippsland SC* (2010)), which deals with developments on floodplains, and *Goulburn Broken Catchment Management Authority v. Cox, Murrindindi Shire Council* (2000). In 2022, however, the Port Phillip and Westernport Catchment Management Authority was integrated into Melbourne Water (*Catchment and Land Protection Act 1994* (Vic) s 11A). The amendments were effected by the *Water and Catchment Legislation Amendment Act 2021* (Vic), which carved out a number of exceptions for Melbourne Water from the application of the Act to other CMAs. The Act also established advisory committees to advise the minister on catchment management and the condition of land and water (s 19AA) and abolished the Victorian Catchment Management Council. In other words, the enactment of the *Yarra River Act 2017* (Vic) replaced one form of legal person with a role in the development of the catchment (the Port Phillip and Westernport Catchment Management Authority) with a new governance framework, the acknowledgement of certain parts of the river and its environs as 'an entity' (not a legal entity) and the integration of the roles of water authority (Melbourne Water) with the previous oversight role of the Catchment Management Authority. The legislative framework also specifically removes significant aspects of the development of city infrastructure from normal planning processes; for instance, the requirement to act consistently with the Yarra Strategic Plan does not apply to a Suburban Rail Loop project within the meaning of the *Suburban Rail Loop Act 2021* (Vic) and projects declared under the *Major Transport Projects Facilitation Act 2009* (Vic). Accordingly, although the Second Reading Speech read at the passage of the Act stated that the Act 'gives the traditional owners a say in the way we plan for and manage the Yarra River and its land', this was the previous position. In the case of both the New Zealand and the Australian experiments, the legislation sets out a framework which is, in expression, entirely at odds with Indigenous experience and worldview. In governance form, both legislative forms continue a project of public sector reform that replaces government oversight of natural resources with responsibilisation of the environment itself (through governance proxy), with the incorporation of an explicit (and newly created) indigenous 'voice' in the governance structure. Indigeneity is drawn into the dominant governance form, rather than sitting outside it as a genuine alternative form.

It is clear that indigenous ontologies provide longstanding localised knowledge and insight into particular ecosystems, as well as providing a corrective lens to the presumptions built into modern legal systems. Further explicit research would be needed to sustain an argument that the insights of indigenous cultures should be preferred to, say, the insights of science, however; or that religious attitudes to the environment would necessarily lead to a preferred environmental outcome. Further, if they are to be more than caveats to a dominant ontology, indigenous ways of dealing with the environment need to be incorporated into legal systems, replace legal systems or elements thereof or be capable of providing practical remedies in a parallel system. In this event, there would inevitably be an assessment of indigenous practices and either acceptance or rejection of their coherence with current scientific knowledge about ecosystems, and more problematically, consistency of indigenous practices with the constraints of current population and settlement requirements.

Colonialism

The recognition of indigenous claims for elements of the environment is, in essence, a response to colonialism; it is no accident that personhood rights are commonly asserted in countries with recent colonial history, and the existence of unaddressed or insufficiently resolved issues of dispossession. Even in nations such as New Zealand, where indigenous law and (loosely described) property rights were acknowledged at the time of European settlement, processes of dispossession continued through disparities in knowledge and power in the sale and purchase of land by settlers. Similar processes of market-based dispossession accompanied the experience of the Anishinaabeg language groups in North America, accompanied by targeted practices aimed at assimilation.

Nevertheless, some critics have identified colonialist aspects of existing environmental strategies – instances in which traditional indigenous interests are directly threatened by environmental interests. Giacomini (2023) reports that the Ogiek Indigenous peoples in Kenya have been forcibly evicted from the Mau Forest Complex to prioritise environmental interests through the creation of Protected Areas. Giacomini attributes the idea of 'uncontaminated nature and wilderness' (Giacomini, 2023, p. 508) underlying the eviction to the 'colonial underpinnings of environmental conservation in Kenya' (Giacomini, 2023, p. 508). A successful action in the African Commission on Human and Peoples' Rights (on the basis that there had been a violation of the African Charter on Human and Peoples' Rights) resulted in an award of monetary damages. In terms of reinstatement of ancestral lands, however, the Court required that collective ownership be conferred through regulatory action – that is, in accordance with the processes set out in legislation. The land demarcation and titling of ancestral lands would require consultation with and the consent of the Ogiek Indigenous peoples in accordance with various international instruments such as the Convention on Biological Diversity

(1992), and in the supplementary agreement, the Nagoya Protocol on Access and Benefit-Sharing (2010) (Article 8(j)) under that Convention. That anti-colonialism is being deployed as an advocacy tool is not without its ironies, therefore. Not only is there a sense in which all Indigenous peoples are assumed to be in alignment with ideas of environmental personhood, but there is also a conflation of meaning in significant concepts. The term 'rights' has a problematic breadth of meaning in Western ontologies and is even more problematic in some indigenous ontologies. The concept of 'rights' in the sense of a bundle of legally enforceable claims in itself is largely a Western construct. This is possibly because such concepts of methods of enforcement were not necessary for indigenous groupings because of small populations and/or abundant resources, or because cultural, religious and legal/enforcement aspects of society were not clearly separated, or it may have been because the individual was entirely subjugated to the family, the tribe or a deity. In many religions, including Christianity, and Catholicism up until the Second Vatican Council, the idea of 'duty' had more traction than the idea of rights. There are dualities and interrelationships with limited traction in Western law and deep divisions between rights concepts in private and public law and in national and international law. The term 'rights' tends to slip between law, philosophy and political advocacy, and the term 'personhood' suffers from the same lack of conceptual clarity. If it is acknowledged that 'rights' can be reposed in a non-human person, further framing must occur to determine not only the extent and enforceability of those rights but also the extent of the 'person' in which the rights are reposed. The way in which individual and community rights are represented and protected in law, the interdependence between (even the lack of separation between) ecosystem elements and humans and even the rights-bearing corpus are subject to interrogation. Hierarchies of rights (and the balancing of different rights claims) will not necessarily track between cultures and legal systems.

The application of the colonial lens over environmental scholarship is not surprising, given its dominance in intellectual (including legal) thought over recent decades. However, attempts to accommodate post-colonial ideas with ecocentrism are not necessarily going to result in a coherent narrative. In particular, post-colonial accounting for the benefits of extractive and agricultural industries and the development infrastructure arising from the use of the environment would be diminished by a markdown to the pre-settlement development condition with ecocentric caveats on exploitation.

Marketisation of natural resources

Drawing upon indigenous ontologies to support ecocentric governance comes up against a well-known issue in literature analysing the rights of Indigenous peoples and in practical politics. Many advocates for the preferencing or acknowledgement of indigenous relationships with the environment place those relationships in contradistinction with contemporary Western, and particularly property- and market-based attitudes to natural resource management (see, e.g. Wardle, 2021). Preferencing particular indigenous worldviews in resource management, particularly in the recognition of resource claims, may limit the scope of Indigenous people to draw upon the environment for their own benefit in modern terms, attracting the criticism that activists are prolonging the wealth disparities created by colonial exploitation. Rights discourse in relation to this has the potential to create a practical cul-de-sac, since Indigenous peoples' rights to development may be inconsistent with the environmentally sensitive practices upon which the argument for recognition of indigenous environmental views relies. Thus, native title recognition in many jurisdictions has more recently moved away from the 'hunting, fishing, and cultural' components of native title recognition to accept some extractive rights. Stride (2022) notes that negotiated settlements of native title claims have moved beyond the outcomes of judicial proceedings to recognise indigenous rights to exploit the natural resources on land and water. How does recognition of the right of Indigenous peoples to utilise natural resources affect the claim of the environment to personhood in its own right? Thus, in terms of the rights of Indigenous peoples, there is a tension between two dominant arguments. First, the assertion that indigenous ways of knowing and experiencing nature should be recognised as uniquely adapted to a particular environment and therefore provide valuable insight into its management is embedded in co-management principles characterising modern legislative responses to this issue. However, confining indigenous interaction with the environment to cultural, religious and social practices pre-dating colonisation will continue historic disadvantage.

If we now parse environmental personhood alongside the rights of Indigenous peoples to flourish through the use of resources to participate in a modern market-based economy, the argument for environmental personhood based on indigenous ontologies becomes problematic. Martinez-Alier (2002, p. 14) describes climate activism as the 'environmentalism of the poor' in the sense that, strategically, the poorest communities can align with environmental groups to bring action to prevent local ecosystem destruction (for instance, through mining or deforestation), which would also have an impact on the livelihoods of the local communities. There may be many instances in which this gives rise to a successful outcome, but there are also many cases in which the impoverished community, once it is empowered, would also wish to utilise its own environment to rise above poverty. This is not necessarily a fatal blow to the compatibility of indigenous and environmental interests; as Angstadt (2016) notes in the context of access to justice, recognition of traditional practices in colonising law and recognition of autonomy within a colonising legal system is highly compatible with environmental personhood where issues of pollution of land and water resources arise, or where resumption of indigenous resources by the state for development interests is posited. Where indigenous rights and capacities to engage in a market economy using natural resources are at issue, however, the conflation of environmental personhood and indigenous ontologies becomes problematic. The most salient representation of this dichotomy can be seen in Ecuador, where, as we have seen, strong constitutional recognition of environmental personhood was almost immediately followed by the expansion of mining activities on the basis that these would increase employment opportunities.

Human representation of environmental interests

If the attribution of rights to nature and its elements is meant, in the words of Kanwal (2023) to create a 'democratic relationship where each constituent has the same value as the other', or a 'dialogue between different epistimologies', then the primary question remaining is one of agency. Who is empowered to speak on behalf of non-human elements, and on what basis does such capacity arise? Once again human agency is relied upon to be a mouthpiece for the environment, giving rise to issues of translation that could replicate the unintended consequences from even well-meaning authors of colonisation. First, it should be noted that the 'environment' does not present a unity of interests any more than humans represent a unity of interests. Whilst different environmental elements may be in balance at a particular time, disruptions to that balance can occur through both natural and anthropogenic influences. Our understanding of the interaction between elements of the environment is growing but remains imperfect. The precautionary principle applies to ensure that lack of full knowledge should not prevent us from taking action to prevent further environmental harm, and in many jurisdictions, this principle is hard-wired into land use planning and environmental protection. However, beyond this principle, which aspect of the environment should be the repository of environmental personhood, so that it stands alongside human interests in resource management? In addition, although humans are part of the environment, it is apparent from the creation of the idea of environmental personhood as a response to the dominance of anthropogenic interests that environmental and human interests may conflict, either in relation to a particular set of humans or humans as a species. In those circumstances, the issue of translation of environmental interests becomes deeply politicised.

Modern co-management principles in the case studies tend to prioritise the insights of groups indigenous to the area. In terms of ecological knowledge, this could perhaps be justified on the basis that indigeneity provides a perspective arising from longevity of observation and cultural knowledge, and certainly this accords with the principle of subsidiarity. This cannot justify every legislative device; the co-planning principles already established by the New Zealand *Resource Management Act* and the incorporation of referral and governance roles in the Victorian legislation typify the consultation processes surrounding resource use and development in many heavily settled countries. In modern frameworks, referencing and accommodation of indigenous ontologies occurs through processes of 'consultation' or 'co-management'. These governance techniques enable a modern state to assert that they are accommodating indigenous ontologies whilst stripping those values of legitimating force and replacing them with modern forms of legitimation. The capacities of indigenous groups to comply with the requirements of these processes and maintain a separate ontological perspective remains an issue, as demonstrated in the Murray-Darling Basin in Australia (Malcolm, 2023). The Northern Basin Aboriginal Nations organisation, which had received funding to enable it to provide advice on indigenous water rights to the Murray-Darling Basin Authority, was defunded on the basis that it did not comply with budgeting, reporting and other governance obligations as required by contract. In the New Zealand context, capacity limitations, including 'lack of skilled people, money and time' (Maxwell et al., 2020, p. 6) have also been noted, and demonstrate that there is a tendency, as a result, to prioritise legislative obligations over non-statutory processes which might resonate more strongly in the Māori community. The governance requirements overlaying the co-management processes might also override indigenous processes; for instance, instituting majority-based rather than collaborative decision-making (Maxwell et al., 2020, p. 6). The techniques of governance typical of a modern state are unlikely to align with the techniques of indigenous communities (or, indeed, many non-indigenous communities) and have the potential to alienate those involved in the process. In the worst case, indigenous co-management could be regarded as a technique of legitimation utilised to divert criticism.

The legitimacy of legal institutions

That modern Western legal systems (broadly construed, noting the extensive cross-fertilisation of legal principles) (Berman, 1978) are based on anthropogenic constructs should be of no particular surprise. Western law is a social construct administered and enforced through institutions formed by and staffed with people. The priorities of these institutions and people will be defined by the documents with which they are created, within the parameters of the nation-state authorising the actions and expenditure of sums of money on these priorities. The institutions are typically funded through taxation, and the justification of taxation is based on techniques of democratic sovereignty, for instance, periodic elections.

The legality of taxation and the consequent disposition of funds according to priorities set by periodic elections is only one aspect of the force of law. Political philosophers have grappled extensively with the basis of the authority and legitimate exercise of law, and bases for constraining the activities of a person range from the use (or potential to use) force through forms of religious authority to the various forms of democratic mandate. The normative status of a form of government, and accordingly of the government's law, will be scaffolded by techniques evolving according to the cultural context; it is common for political regimes to harness cultural devices to support their own power and authority to rule. Accordingly, the various dimensions of local culture are deeply imprinted on the politics and law of a particular region, unless wholesale cultural reform has occurred by invasion or revolution (violent, cultural or scientific). The utilisation of mechanisms of force (such as expropriation of natural assets) or public expenditure for purposes which do not have sufficient cultural grounding constitutes a risk to the stability of the state. One of the strategies of advocates for change is to attract sufficient public support to change the culture of the society gradually enough that this is not a risk to stability. Even then there will be groups of people who will adapt more slowly and will be damaged in the process. The English *Inclosure Acts* between the 1600s and the 1900s, which created property rights to land out of common or 'waste' land with a view to increasing the food supply, displaced many rural people. The Acts themselves replaced the depopulation of the countryside by turning it over to sheep pasturage rights. These revolutionary shifts, still debated, in the utilisation of land in England, occurred through a series of legislative provisions which converted customary into legally recognisable property rights. Although it could be said that the English form of democracy of the time was not perfect, it was at least utilising an open forum, using reasoned argument, subject to continuous oversight and open to public criticism.

It should be noted that the perceptions of legitimacy will generally increase in accordance with an iterative process of education and reinforcement, as well as the success of the state in maintaining the safety and well-being of its citizens. Thus, where a state tends towards instability, as in the case of Ecuador, the legitimacy of law is as problematic as the legitimacy of the state. In the case of Ecuador, despite the fact that the Constitution was formulated by a broadly democratic process, democracy is not trusted – surveys show that in 2023 only 37% of people believed in democracy as a form of governance (Latinobarómetro, 2023, p. 25). Thus, although Ecuador apparently has the strongest theoretical frameworks for environmental personhood, the constitution and the system of government generally is one of the most fragile of the countries which have introduced environmental personhood. Introducing a novel form of personhood in modern democracies is reliant on robust forms of legitimacy, which are yet to have yielded the strong statement of personhood in Ecuador. Conversely, the strong statement of environmental personhood in Ecuador is based on a fragile document and is poorly grounded in perceived legitimate form.

Conversely, where litigation has been used to advance revolutionary change, it could be criticised as bypassing democratic processes altogether. One of the risks of litigation as a mechanism to drive major systemic change is that the court system is not designed to ground and legitimise social change and it is ill-adapted to be a consultative mechanism. It could, of course, be argued that the court system is in itself supported by and legitimated by the socio-political context in which it exists, and even if it is not required to rule on the validity or application of legislation (which has been subject to democratic oversight), it will still consider the consequences of creating a judicial precedent which will create uncertainty or undermine key principles of law.

One of these key principles is the separation of powers between the judiciary and the legislature. High-profile climate cases such as *Urgenda Foundation v. State of the Netherlands* have been criticised on the basis that the judiciary impermissibly undertook a legislative role. In that case, the Urgenda foundation, which had been created to 'stimulate and accelerate the transition to a more sustainable society, starting with the Netherlands' (Meguro, 2020, p. 729), brought an action against the Dutch government in the District Court of the Hague (Rechtbank) based on obligations under the European Convention on Human Rights Article 2 and 8 seeking an order that it reduce greenhouse gas emissions by at least 25% of the 1990 level by 2020. Unsuccessful initially and on appeal to the Court of Appeal (Gerechtshof) (*Urgenda Foundation v. State of the Netherlands*, 2018), an appeal to the Supreme Court held that Articles 2 and 8 applied to the emission of greenhouse gas emissions and that the state could be responsible for failing to take appropriate measures to reduce emissions (*Urgenda Foundation v. State of the Netherlands*, 2019). The Court of Appeal expressly addressed criticism of an activist court, dismissing it on the basis that a judge is democratically supported by legislation establishing the court, and that certain legal actions – for instance, cases seeking relief against administrative decision-making – confer a protective role on the judiciary. Criticism based on the effect of the decision on the separation of powers has noted the potential for unintended consequences: 'the idea of a world rescue through court decisions is ultimately misleading … it shifts responsibilities and creates expectations that tend to further de-legitimize the constitutional democratic systems of the world and their concept of a separation of powers' (Wegener, 2019, p. 125).

Urgenda is considered extraordinary for several reasons (not all related to issues of judicial law-making) and it is not reflected in cases elsewhere: in *Greenpeace Norway v. Norwegian State*, the Oslo District Court refused to hear an action by a youth organisation on that basis. In Australia, the Full Court of the Federal Court in *Minister for the Environment v. Sharma* (2022) emphasised the unsuitability of the court to assess policy decisions. The case, and others like it, raises a common issue in judicial oversight of government decisions – common law courts do have a jurisdiction to oversee government decision-making, but are reluctant to intervene in 'policy', as opposed to 'operational' decision-making. A postscript to the *Sharma* case demonstrates an alternative strategy. After the conclusion of litigation, advocates lobbied independent Senator David Pocock to introduce a private member's Bill to amend the Australian federal *Climate Change Act 2022* (Cth) by creating a duty of care owed by governments to consider the impact on young people of decisions which would significantly increase greenhouse gas emissions.

Strategic advocacy follows an 'all-fronts' approach, utilising a range of legal tools and approaches regardless of the traditional purpose of the law. Thus, although it would be legally sound to approach cases using planning or municipal law to overturn individual decisions, and many cases are heard in these jurisdictions, decisions of this type are less valuable from a strategic perspective since they are specific to location and local laws, and in some cases, have little to no weight as precedents. The administrative law context is highly appropriate since the purpose of administrative law is to ensure that the decisions of public authorities are made on appropriate grounds, using appropriate materials. The weakness of this jurisdiction is that the authority's decision will not be successfully challenged when it is legitimately made on the basis of the legislation. Environmental advocates may, in fact, have taken issue with the legislation, and are seeking to attack it through litigation rather than through political channels.

Cases which challenge the law on constitutional grounds either seek to apply constitutional provisions more widely than their previously understood scope or seek reform of a widespread and fundamental character. Some constitutions contain specific environmental rights, although these are generally more modern instruments. Older constitutions do not tend to have this level of detail and have not generally adopted content from the rights framework developed in the United Nations, as have the Indian and Ecuadorian constitutions. Where no constitutional reference to the environment exists, a successful constitutional claim can potentially have wide-reaching effects on the powers of the legislature and potentially disrupt a federal balance of powers: *Tasmanian Dams case* (1983), *Richardson v. Forestry Commission (Lemonthyme Forests case)* (1988) and the *Tropical Rainforests case* (1989) contributed to the centralisation of power under the Australian federal constitution that marked a fundamental change to the legal and political infrastructure of the country. It could be argued that a fundamental change to the balance of federal power should more properly be the subject of a referendum, although this argument triggers the 'living document' versus 'originalist' debate in constitutional circles (see, for instance, Miller, 2009; Post & Siegel, 2006).

Litigation in private law will occur based on the selection of a case which could yield a powerful precedent. Common law negligence (a case based on a failure of a person owing a duty of care to comply with the standard of a reasonable person, thus causing damage) has been an attractive tort for strategic litigation since a case authority which finds that a duty of care is owed will have broad application. The salient issue arising with litigation in private law is that the law chosen for strategic focus may well be ill-adapted to a resolution of the question and, if successful, the matter may lead to incoherence or inconsistency in the law. The tort of nuisance is most appropriate in terms of remedy for cases involving environmental harm; however, it is highly contextual – cases turn on their own facts – and thus will often not lead to wider application. The strategic focus on the tort of negligence, currently seeking to litigate to a precedent which finds decision-makers owe a duty of care to 'future generations' for environmental harm, widens the tort into areas of law more appropriately governed by the tort of nuisance or breach of statutory duty or administrative actions.

References

Angstadt, J. M. (2016). Securing access to justice through environmental courts and tribunals: A case in diversity. *Vermont Journal of Environmental Law*, *17*(3), 345.

Angstadt, J. M. & Hourdequin, M. (2021). Taking Stock of the Rights of Nature in D. P. Corrigan & M. Oksanen (Eds.), *Rights of Nature – A Re-examination*. London: Routledge.

Berman, H. J. (1978). Background of the Western legal tradition in the Folklaw of the peoples of Europe. *University of Chicago Law Review*, *45*(3), 553.

Cajete, G. (2000). *Native science: Natural laws of interdependence*. Clear Light Publishers.

Chaturvedi, I. (2019) Why the Ganga should not claim a right of the river. *Water International*, *44*(6–7), 719–735.

Climate Change Act 2022 (Cth).

Commonwealth v. Tasmania (Tasmanian Dam case) (1983) 158 CLR 1.

Dancer, H. (2021). Harmony with Nature: Towards a new deep legal pluralism. *Journal of Legal Pluralism and Unofficial Law*, *53*(1), 21–41.

Ewering, E. S., & Vetter, T. (2023). Making nature invisible. Procedural limits and possibilities of environmental litigation. In A. Fischer-Lescano & A. V. Franco (Eds.), *Nature as a subject of rights: A philosophical and legal dialogue between Germany and Ecuador* Unikassel Versitat.

Giacomini, G. (2023). Human rights violations in the name of environmental protection: Reflections on the reparations owed to the Ogiek Indigenous people of Kenya. *Ordine Internazionale e Diritti Umani*, *3*, 508–520.

Greenpeace. Norway v. Norwegian State (2018, January 4). Oslo District Court, Case No.16-166674TVI-OTIR/06.

Goulburn Broken Catchment Management Authority v. Cox, Murrindindi Shire Council & Ors [2000] VicPRp 29.

Hams, S. (2023, June 21). Woman who fatally stabbed mother at Kilburn home jailed for manslaughter. *ABC News* [Online]. https://www.abc.net.au /news/2023-06-21/woman-jailed-for-fatal-stabbing-of-mother-at-kilburn /102504848

Israel, J. (2006). *Enlightenment contested: Philosophy, modernity, and the emancipation of man 1670–1752*. OUP.

Kanwal, P. (2023). Ecocentric governance: Recognising the rights of nature. *Indian Journal of Public Administration*, 1–13. https://doi.org/10.1177 /00195561221141457

Latinobarómetro. (2023). *Report: The democratic recession in Latin America*. Latinobarómetro Corporation.

Malcolm, J. (2023, August 17). Murray-Darling: Cash for wisdom on water wasted. *The Australian*.

Martinez-Alier, J. (2002). *The environmentalism of the poor: A study of ecological conflicts and valuation*. Edward Elgar.

Maxwell, K., Awatere, S., Ratana, K., Davies, K., & Taiapa, C. (2020). He waka eke noa/we are all in the same boat: A framework for co-governance from Aotearoa New Zealand. *Marine Policy*, *121*, 104213.

Meguro, M. (2020). State of the Netherlands v Urgenda Foundation. *American Journal of International Law*, *114*(4), 729.

Michael, A. J., & Hourdequin, M. (2021). Taking stock of the rights of nature. In P. Corrigan Daniel & M. Oksanen (Eds.), *Rights of nature - a re-examination* (pp. 14–35). Routledge.

Miller, B. W. (2009). Beguiled by metaphors: The "living tree" and originalist constitutional interpretation in Canada. *Canadian Journal of Law and Jurisprudence*, *22*(2), 331–354.

Minister for the Environment v. Sharma [2022] FCAFC 35.

Norman, E. S. (2017). Standing up for inherent rights: The role of indigenous-led activism in protecting sacred waters and ways of life. *Society and Natural Resources*, *30*(4), 537–553. https://doi.org/10.1080/08941920.2016 .1274459

Post, R., & Siegel, R. (2006). Originalism as a political practice: The right's living constitution. *Fordham Law Review, 75*(2), 545.

Queensland v. Clth (Tropical Rainforests case) (1989) 167 CLR 232.

Richardson v. Forestry Commission (1988) 164 CLR 261.

Rose, D. B. (1996). *Nourishing terrains: Australian Aboriginal views of landscape and wilderness.* Australian Heritage Commission.

Schimmöller, L. (2020). Paving the way for rights of nature in Germany: Lessons learnt from legal reform in New Zealand and Ecuador. *Transnational Environmental Law, 9*(3), 569–592.

Singh, P. (2010). The scandal of enlightenment and the birth of disciplines: Is international law a science? *International Community Law Review, 12*(1), 5–34. https://doi.org/10.1163/187197410X12631788215792

State of the Netherlands v. Urgenda Foundation, ECLI:NL:HR:2019:2007, Judgment (Sup. Ct. Neth. Dec. 20, 2019) (Neth.).

Thomas, J. A. C. (1963). Custom and Roman law. *Tijdschrift voor Rechtsgeschiedenis/Legal History Review, 31*(1), 39.

Urgenda Foundation v. The State of the Netherlands (2018, October 9). Court of Appeal, The Hague, (Neth.) ECLI:NL:GHDHA:2018:2610.

Wardle, D. (2021). Sustainable indigenous water rights. In J. C. Spee, A. McMurray, & M. McMillan (Eds.), *Clan and tribal perspectives on social, economic and environmental sustainability* (pp. 9–22). Emerald Publishing Limited. https://doi.org/10.1108/978-1-78973-365-520211003

Wegener, B. (2019). Urgenda - World rescue by court order? The "Climate Justice" movement tests the limits of legal protection. *Journal for European Environmental and Planning Law. 16*, 125–147.

West Gippsland Catchment Management Authority v. East Gippsland SC [2010] VCAT 1334 (August 4, 2010).

West Gippsland Catchment Management Authority v. South Gippsland SC [2017] VCAT 63 (January 10, 2017).

White, H. (2018). Indigenous peoples, the international trend toward legal personhood for nature, and the United States. *American Indian Law Review, 43*, 129. https://digitalcommons.law.ou.edu/ailr/vol43/iss1/4

Yoorrook Justice Commission. (2023). *Yoorrook for justice: Report into Victoria's child protection and criminal justice systems.* Parliament of Victoria.

Chapter 5

Conclusions

Epstein et al. argue that '[r]ights-of-nature laws have reached a critical point at which they may either be normalized or marginalized. They have captured the public imagination, leading to growing advocacy for, and enactment of, these laws' (Epstein et al., 2023, p. 380). In itself, this could be considered a success, in the sense that environmental advocates managed to gain significant market share in a crowded attention economy. The movement is maturing, and the current strategy of advocates is to build upon the United Nations Resolution that a healthy environment is a human right (UN, 2022) and to argue for a right to legal personhood for nature. The preceding discussion, therefore, only provides a glimpse of the contentions to come. This concluding chapter reframes rights discourse in its philosophical context and then considers the sustainability of a bespoke legal framework for the protection of the environment in the context of a political and legal system brokered by human interests. Those working towards recognising, or utilising, concepts of environmental personhood are motivated by real and increasing concerns for the current and future world.

As we have seen, there is a complex set of potentially conflicting philosophical, jurisprudential and practical issues confronting advocates for environmental personhood. Whilst these issues are not insurmountable, since personhood is conceptually fluid, this is also a problem. Legal personhood as a construct delivers no more protection than is enabled by a particular legal system at a particular time. At its most problematic, the responsibilisation of the environment for the protection of its own rights (even if by proxy) encourages an anthropocentric view of environmental rights, atomises the environmental whole (which includes human animals) into disparate and potentially antagonistic parts and discourages thinking that incorporates the environment and its humans as a symbiotic and interactive complex. If limited attributes of personhood are reposed in the environment in much the same way as they are reposed on a corporation, the adoption

DOI: 10.4324/9781003388272-5

of forms of personhood in diluted form also risks the type of narrative greenwashing too often seen in political and corporate responses to environmental concerns. Conversely, the relevance of the rights of nature to improve environmental outcomes has not been established (Wesche, 2021, p. 533).

If we take a step back to consider the traditional mechanisms for the protection of non-human nature and its elements, it should be acknowledged that there are many legal, political and economic tools currently deployed to address issues of pollution, overallocation and resource depletion and to address climate change (McDonald, 2011). Some of these tools are longstanding and have been successful in mitigating pollution in the past. In common law countries, we have seen that the tort of nuisance, for instance, can be utilised to prevent polluting uses of lands. It has its origins in common law and, as Winfield (1931) notes, was legally defined very early in legal history. The capacity of the tort to protect nature per se is incidental, as it developed primarily to protect a person's use or enjoyment of land in which they had an interest. This speaks to the anthropocentrism of the law generally, but as the United Nations' acceptance of a human right to a healthy environment articulates, human and environmental interests are aligned. The common law, developing incrementally as it does, accommodates this view – nuisance has developed to serve wider interests and has been utilised to protect environmental ends. Other torts are developing along similar lines. The tort of negligence, for instance, has been utilised in many jurisdictions to move beyond the individual owed a duty to protect. Recent cases have assayed (largely unsuccessfully) the capacity of the tort to address systemic issues such as climate change. Contract law and property law are central to the creation of the market for ecosystem services, water trading, carbon credits and other tools for mitigation. Planning law, which is typically based on local legislation and considers the environment in a local but interactive context, is a powerful tool for environmental advocacy as well as the consideration of indigenous interests, as it usually contains structural bases for public participation. This grounds planning decision-making in both the democratic authority of state and delegated legislation and also in the place-based participation of the local community. Legitimacy is afforded by traditional mechanisms.

Advocates of environmental personhood argue that traditional law, grounding the environment in property law, regulates the exploitation of the environment, rather than protecting it (Spitz & Penalver, 2021). However, this contention could be disputed, as could the usefulness of environmental personhood as a solution. As Spitz and Penalver (2021, p. 71) note about the unsuccessful attempt to use litigation to have the Colorado River given the status of legal person (*Colorado River Ecosystem v. Colorado*, 2017), the plaintiffs overstated the dichotomy between personhood and property law, simultaneously exaggerating the potential for personhood to bring meaningful change to the Colorado River's existing comanagement system and undervaluing the rich and varied property relationships possible within the common law conception of ownership ... the plaintiff displayed too little appreciation of the potential of legal tools existing within property law (e.g., conservation easements, trusts, etc.), and too much faith in legal personhood to do the hard work of fundamentally changing how human beings interact with the Colorado River. This may have been a litigation strategy, but the failure to acknowledge the potential for property law positioned the case as oppositional to progressive property law litigation and likely hurt the plaintiff's credibility with the court.

At a political level, the creation, utilisation or oversight of public agencies with the obligation to provide the sort of protection sought by environmental advocates would appear to be the most appropriate solution to the issues addressed by environmental personhood. Since, in all cases, personhood reposed in the environment will need human agents to interpret, prioritise and implement protective actions, why put the environment on the same level as an individual person, required to advocate for its own protection? Ignoring or seeking to bypass the obvious strategy of creating (or utilising) a body legislatively required to protect the environment signals distrust in the institutional solution or impatience with the efforts of current institutions. This is certainly the sense in which much of the discourse occurs: existing institutional mechanisms are 'characterized in terms of a nexus of capitalism, liberal democracy, and the administrative state' (Dryzek, 1992, p. 18), which are 'thoroughly inept with it comes to ecology' (Dryzek, 1992, p. 19). Where legislative mechanisms have created personhood (or the less striking 'living entity') status in the environment, however, these bodies are also embedded to an extent in the legislative and administrative framework; in particular, in the problem of ensuring funding on a regular basis. In some countries, particular institutional issues have been identified; Wardana notes that in Indonesia there is a lack of public engagement with the issue of climate change, and whereas courts may rule against illegal loggers, the economy will frequently be prioritised over concerns about coal-generated power (Wardana, 2023, p. 367).

Given the various existing avenues for the protection of the environment, including existing legal techniques, the next question is the appropriateness of using law (particularly litigation) as an advocacy tool. Various arguments draw upon different views as to the proper role of law in society, so again this is by necessity a brief outline of the issues. Once again it demonstrates a divergence of underlying philosophies depending on the understanding of the nature and authority of law. Of course, all law has elements of advocacy either in its creation or its enforcement; but when advocacy for fundamental change bypasses democratic processes, wider questions arise, including issues of separation between judicial and legislative power (Burgers, 2020). The environmental personhood movement expresses the perceived need for a thorough transformation of institutions, including the law itself. Is this a form of advocacy that strikes at the heart of legal institutions – at the law itself? Does it in fact amount to the form of civil disobedience from which lawyers may be ethically disbarred (Palumbos, 2005), or are lawyers, by advocating fundamental change, demonstrating respect for the law? Environmental advocates can quite cogently argue that corporations have been utilising forms of advocacy as a matter of strategy, including canvassing political support, selecting cases to create precedent and paying settlements to avoid the creation of precedent, use of 'strategic litigation against public participation (SLAPP)' and funding of political parties and groups favourable to their interests. One only has to consider the role of insurance companies, themselves a major component of international financial systems, in selecting, arguing and settling cases. In essence, environmental advocates are mirroring the same strategies. However, traditional legal analysis clearly requires the governing body of a corporation to prioritise shareholders in decision-making, so corporate utilisation of SLAPP strategies is justifiable and appropriately addressed through anti-SLAPP legislation or legislation governing corporate gifts. Conversely, the primary duties of a lawyer are to the law and the courts.

Cole (1995) points to the use of litigation in a particular legal system (using local planning issues as a case study) as a technique to resolve the 'inequitable distribution of environmental hazards' (the environmental justice argument). However, he points to the 'strategic use of public participation provisions in [existing] environmental laws' (Cole, 1995, p. 689). He notes that using an approach which recognises the imbalances of power in decision-making, and strategically deploying influence within that system, 'teaches its adherents to distrust the system, while also teaching them how to use that system' (Cole, 1995, p. 707). It is a form of empowering the powerless. Similarly, the strategies of environmental advocates include the accumulation of legal precedent (Kauffman & Martin, 2017, p. 136) and the goal of informing and 'training' decision-makers (Kauffman & Martin, 2017, p. 131). In a similar vein, Wesche argues that attribution of legal personhood is less about overcoming legal barriers such as standing, and more about strengthening governance frameworks, particularly in countries with weak governance capabilities. In countries with 'strong institutions, strong rule of law and a well-functioning legal system, which greatly relies on private law damages in regulating grievances that are elsewhere rather addressed in public law litigation' (Wesche, 2021, p. 554), it could be argued that rights of nature could lead to practical legal outcomes, but countries with weak governance capacities, 'dysfunctional state institutions and absence of rule of law in many areas affected by grave environmental damage'(Wesche, 2021, p. 554), the role of rights of nature advocacy amounts to a 'transformative public policy-oriented approach', leading to a 'productive interplay' (Wesche, 2021, p. 554) with symbolic effects rather than concrete outcomes. This could be reformulated to the effect that in countries with strong legal systems and good governance, environmental personhood is effective legally, but not really necessary given the alternative legal recourse available. In countries with weak legal and governance systems, environmental personhood is legally ineffective but may have an influence over time on governance systems.

More ambitiously, Mussawir and Parsley (2017) argue that the movement to create different ideas of personhood is a 'return to a casuistic, concrete and immanent conception of the jurisprudential art of crafting the person' (Mussawir & Parsley, 2017, p. 46). In their account of the historical account of legal personhood, the authors do note the 'functional and circumscribed conception of the person' in Roman jurisprudence (Mussawir & Parsley, 2017, p. 46), and the perception of critical legal scholarship of the need to

> take a wrecking-ball, if not just to the edifice of the 'legal subject' then also to the strict juridical conception of the person – the abstract formalism of which it has commonly taken as a mask simply for the dominant forms of power.
>
> (Mussawir & Parsley, 2017, p. 61)

Claiming personhood for non-persons is, accordingly, more than probing and stretching the boundaries of traditional legal categories. It is a continuation of the disruption of the marginalising fictions of law itself. The question is, if activists undermine the legitimacy of law in forwarding their environmental goals, they are risking an imperfectly legitimised legal system and the attendant potential for state failure.

That said, the stated goals of advocates for environmental personhood suggest that the movement, if realistically aiming for success, would experience longer-term issues dealing with questions of priority between human and ecosystem elements in periods of genuine human crisis. Maintaining support for ecosystem elements when the economy is in a downturn and ecosystem priorities overrule the expansion of economic opportunities is difficult, as we see in the case of Ecuador. If full civic personhood is suggested, other issues arise. The concept(s) of personhood in the sense(s) understood by law and legal systems are bound so closely to capacities to express consent, by which process law and legal systems are tolerated by those subjected to them. Alternatives exist, of course. Brute force is a well-established mechanism for the support of a legal system, as are money, status, religious edict and mythology. Many states are maintained by corruption, nepotism and the brutal suppression of alternative views. We should be wary of enabling these states to assert that they are, in some sense, acting for the mute environment to justify their actions.

Rather than reaching for the (perhaps utopian) goal, it is arguable that modern attributions of environmental personhood are, in Butler's sense, a subversive use of performativity – using the language of legal personhood to 'reinscribe' the term (in the Derridian sense) (Butler, 2021, pp. 144–145). Butler suggests that the 'political promise' of catachresis – in this case, redeploying the term 'legal personhood' in the context of a vague and shifting environment – is in its 'insurrectionary potential' (Butler, 2021, p. 145). The arguments tend to avoid the ontological consequences (especially for traditional conceptions of law) and utilise arguments directed at relational personhood which originate in critique, particularly critique of neo-liberalism. Law, however, is not a product of neo-liberalism, and although legal forms have been utilised to progress the market, particularly in laws relating to contract and property, that is not their only or even their primary goal. Whilst we may revisit Banner's critique of the black letter legal view that '[law] does not intervene in markets; law constitutes markets' (Banner, 2000, p. 50), and note that law was a tool for and symbol of colonisation, the market, in the sense of the capacity to trade (that is, contract), is an ancient construct and inherent in the capacity of people to form settled communities. Legal forms to protect property (and the yields of labour) are fundamental to the safety of a settled community. In subverting legal forms and celebrating the successes represented by legislation and cases that have accepted the idea of environmental personhood, there is presumably no real intention to undermine accepted ideas of representative democracy and the laws of property and contract, although disruptive anthropogenic ideas of law would have that effect. It is unclear, however, what is to be the real end point. What is clear is that in the different mechanisms for reposing personhood on elements of the environment, we are seeing the culmination of a reorientation of 'rights' over time.

References

Banner, S. (2000). Conquest by contract: wealth transfer and land market structure in colonial New Zealand. *Law & Society Review, 34*(1), 47.

Burgers, L. (2020). Should judges make climate change law? *Transnational Environmental Law, 9*(1), 55–75.

Butler, J. (2021). *Excitable speech: A politics of the performative*. Routledge.

Cole, L. W. (1995). Macho law brains, public citizens, and grassroots activists: Three models of environmental advocacy. *Virginia Environmental Law Journal*, *14*(4), 687.

Colorado River Ecosystem v. Colorado (2017). 1 p. 17-cv-02316 (D. Colo. Sept. 25, 2017).

Dryzek, J. S. (1992). Ecology and discursive democracy: Beyond liberal capitalism and the administrative state. *Capitalism, Nature, Socialism*, *3*(2), 18–42.

Epstein, Y., Ellison, A. M., Echeverría, H., & Abbott, J. K. (2023). Science and the legal rights of nature. *Science*, *380*(6646).

Kauffman, Craig M., & Martin, Pamela L. (2017). Can rights of nature make development more sustainable? Why some Ecuadorian lawsuits succeed and others fail. *World Development*, *92*, 130–142.

McDonald, J. (2011). The role of law in adapting to climate change. *WIREs Climate Change*, *2*(2), 283. https://doi.org/10.1002/wcc.96

Mussawir, E., & Parsley, C. (2017). The law of persons today: At the margins of jurisprudence. *Law and Humanities*, *11*(1), 44–63. https://doi.org/10.1080/17521483.2017.1320041

Palumbos, R. M. (2005). Within each lawyer's conscience a touchstone: Law, morality, and attorney civil disobedience. *University of Pennsylvania Law Review*, *153*(3), 1057.

Spitz, L., & Penalver, E. M. (2021). Nature's personhood and property's virtues. *Harvard Environmental Law Review*, *45*(1), 67.

United Nations, A/Res/76/300 [New York]: UN, July 26, 2022.

Wardana, A. (2023). Governing through courts? Law and the political-economy of climate change litigation in Indonesia. *Verfassung und Recht in Übersee*, *56*(2), 351–370.

Wesche, P. (2021). Rights of nature in practice: A case study on the impacts of the Colombian Atrato River Decision. *Journal of Environmental Law*, *33*(3), 531–555.

Winfield, P. H. (1931). Nuisance as a tort. *Cambridge Law Journal*, *4*(2), 189–206.

Index

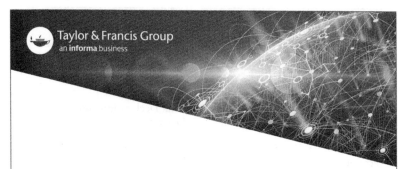